D1587129

Picasso says . . .

# Picasso says . . .

BY HÉLÈNE PARMELIN

TRANSLATED BY CHRISTINE TROLLOPE

London
GEORGE ALLEN AND UNWIN LTD

Translated from the French *Picasso dit ...*
© 1966, Editions Gonthier, Paris

PRINTED IN GREAT BRITAIN
*in 11 on 13 pt. Juliana*
BY WESTERN PRINTING SERVICES LTD, BRISTOL

*'I do not say everything, but I paint everything . . .'*
February 21st, 1966

# Note

All the sentences in italics are Picasso's.
Those placed between inverted commas are exact
reproductions of his words. The others reproduce
them almost exactly as he uttered them.

# Contents

# Contents

Contents

# Picasso
# the painter

Picasso said: '*We must kill modern art.*'

It was not the first time that sentence had prowled around Notre-Dame de Vie. But never had it taken on so imperious and uncompromising an air as it did on that winter evening in 1965.

'*It means, too*', said Picasso, '*that we must kill ourselves if we want to go on accomplishing anything.*'

That's the hardest thing to do, to kill oneself. The painter gets caught on his own bristles. Try as he may, habit goes on guiding his hand.

But the moment comes when, unless he is to get lost, he must turn back on himself like a dog chasing its tail. The dog always catches the same dog. '*Still, it doesn't always catch it by the same end,*' as Picasso says.

He often stresses the fact that a painter who is not constantly in revolt against his own *a priori* attitudes is lost.

So he is in revolt against Picasso; it is Picasso he aims to kill. To kill him as a painter kills; that is to say in such a way that the essential is left, like those little lead-weighted figures which can be turned or pushed down in any direction, and always spring into an upright position again.

Thus we must '*kill modern art*'.

There was a time when Picasso never tired of uttering that sentence and in his own way putting it into effect, and at that moment he finished 'The painter and his model'.

That is, actually, a completely inaccurate way of putting it,

15

He finished nothing at all. It is always a mistake to consider a period that has been 'exhibited' as 'finished'. It is the work that comes afterwards, continuing the same period, the work born too late to be caught between the walls of the exhibition gallery, that is to become the most important.

So let us simply say that the exhibition 'The painter and his model' took place, and that the canvases made conquests. Particularly among painters; and that, for Picasso, is still '*the thing that counts most*'.

But not only among painters. The press blew a mighty fanfare of triumph and fulsome praise. Never had there been an exhibition like it; Picasso, they said, overwhelmed everything with his vitality, his invention, his inspired craftsmanship. All that was liveliest, boldest and most brilliant in painting exploded into life in his canvases and showed us the way . . . And so on.

The exhibition 'The painter and his model' was thus a real triumph for Picasso all along the line.

Triumphs, when they burst upon us, are sweet (Who can deny it? Does everybody enjoy being attacked?) Perhaps they also put a little soothing balm on the hundred thousand stab wounds in the back which the world inflicts on Picasso every day. (And in comparison the triumphs are so few . . .)

But at the same time such favour irritates the painter. For it rises in the place he has already left. Or so he says. He is no longer to be reached at that particular point in his work. He is already elsewhere.

When Paris is quivering with his triumph—if triumph there is—Picasso is far beyond the exhibition which has just begun. The canvases that go to make it are already the past for him. Even if, like anyone else—any painter—he feels apprehension or curiosity to see his work rubbing shoulders with the public, he already longs for a different, an impossible confrontation with yet another work—his present one.

It is not only that he has moved on. If perchance he wonders anxiously how the world is reacting to his canvases, he is

16

thinking of those on which he is working at present. And those no one but his wife has yet seen.

Those are the ones he would like people to see. Not the old ones, those old yesterday's canvases that are being exhibited. It is the new ones whose effect he longs to measure on the eyes of the world, the terrible eyes of the crowd, the only true eyes and the only false, the most cruel and the most prone to error, but those with which the struggle must be waged.

What is more, he gives the impression that starting from his current canvases he has discovered things to which his finished canvases, that have flown far away from his studio, had given him no more than the key. His true invention, his great discovery, is even now being born at Notre-Dame de Vie.

I seem to be losing myself among the painter's anxieties. But what greater truth is there? And what more admirable? (Especially when we are speaking of Picasso, of whom it might be thought that he is not very interested in the impact of his canvases on the world and *vice versa*. Actually the opposite is true, to his great glory).

True painters can never rest on their laurels. They can only live the unending, terrible life of painters, fighting the battle of painting to the bitter end. A painter is never satisfied.

'But the worst thing of all', says Picasso, 'is that he has never finished. There is never a moment when you can say "I've done a good day's work and tomorrow is Sunday." As soon as you stop you have to start again. You can put aside a canvas and say you won't touch it any more. But you can never write the words THE END.'

At the heart of this perpetual non-tranquillity is a swarming mass of ideas, and every one of them a wombful of canvases. Something reaches completion, or appears to. And everything else both springs from and works against this very

17

thing. The work contains its own truth, but chiefly it conceals within itself a springboard from which, turning our back on it, we can fly to the discovery of a new truth, the very reverse of the first. It is after all quite normal that in painting as in everything else we should come to deny what once seemed the foundation of all truth, so true that we thought it could never be doubted again.

'And in the end', said Picasso, 'when the work is there, the painter has already gone.'

For (as he said another day) 'the painter is never the same thing as the style'.

How many painters are consigned to a living death, idolized, exhibited, hung in galleries all over the world, sold by every dealer, written about, reproduced, an unending, identical reflection of themselves, wearing a style, a manner, a way of working, like a strait-jacket?

Picasso says 'I no longer want reality in my forms. If I did I should be like a pastry-cook making moulds and beating up all sorts of mixtures to put into them. One flavoured with ginger, another with pistachio. After that you wouldn't dare to put one foot out of your mould.'

Anyway people are generally satisfied with styles; they find in them the security they want. There is nothing more soothing than an *avant-garde* style, immovably set in its own mould, universally recognized and catalogued as such.

I am trying to restore the climate of conversations with Picasso, which when they touch on painting are always dominated by a certain passion. I am trying to give the atmosphere if the not the words, of which only certain ones remain in the memory. I am trying to bring to life a Picasso-truth, a painter-truth, by writing round these conversations between four people, one of whom was a painter—which is extremely important. I am recording the conversations of painters about painting. Plus the Model, who lives painting and can talk about it from the inside.

Picasso, then, declares that we must kill modern art 'since, once again, modern is just what it no longer is'.

Not only does this notion of modernity become out of date as time flashes by, but we no longer even know what it means. In painting it breaks through the sound barrier, and we haven't any of us got over our amazement at seeing the modernity of abstract art toppled by the double boom of action painting, abstract expressionism, and other aberrations, and then the next day painting finds itself with a great comic-strip head, which is pop art, and a body modestly blurred, which is the new style of representation, with the constant winking of op art and the futile gossip of narrative figuration.

Which of these was modern?

In any case they are all contemporary.

'But it isn't a question of terms,' says Picasso. 'It isn't this or that aspect of modern art that we have to kill. Why should we—and which one?'

Because if you think what has been going on in 1964 or 1965 ... There's a bit of everything, under every possible name. There are luminous canvases that fade out with the projectors, moving canvases in the manner of Loie Fuller, great heads of funny men and little pop paintings. People are sticking on bits and pieces, cutting holes, sculpture-painting and architecture-painting, interior decorating, making mobiles and collages, caricaturing, refining, painting to scale, and on occasion collectivising the whole lot. They're also doing very large pictures.

At the same time they are still making very pretty contrivances which move in an extremely pleasing way, and which, amid all this hotch-potch of limelight, electric fires with artificial flames, and bits of newspaper, give one a certain mechanical satisfaction. They work. They actually turn round. It's all very pretty and very fascinating.

But one night in summer, coming back from Notre-Dame de Vie after a short stay all on my own, which had been very fertile in thoughts of all kinds, I was waiting on the station platform and watching the regular movement of an engine's connecting rods. How ordered it was! And how beautiful! Just like those charming contraptions I was talking about. That's what I said to myself.

Only, in this case it adds up to a railway engine.

I know the absurd contrivance works all the same, and that its connecting rods, or whatever, turn perfectly, all for nothing . . . and it isn't really nothing, either.

But as soon as one gets near Picasso's studio and the climate of his life, everything flows once more with sap and sapience, and everything that plays with art in the slightest degree drops out of fashion and is sent packing.

I would like to emphasise the fact that the things I have just said—which are absolutely necessary if I am to continue my account and at the same time show how Picasso's present researches are motivated—do not come from him, and are not summaries of his thought. I am not Picasso's interpreter. No one is. Nor his mouthpiece.

I am simply endeavouring to situate his researches as they are at the moment in the actual climate created by the international situation of the moment in art. If these few landmarks were not there I could show Picasso evolving in Picasso and through Picasso, but not Picasso wielding his sword in the battle of his time.

All the more because he belongs passionately to his time, and all the changing fortunes of painting claim his attention. Everything spurs him on. Or wounds him. But at any rate everything interests him. His only isolation is that of work.

On the day of the private view of his exhibition 'The painter and his model' in the Louise Leiris Gallery at Kahnweiler's, he said on the telephone, using his familiar formula, that '*he had done thousands more since then*'.

But that they were already '*something quite different*'.

He painted four or five, six or seven canvases a day, not counting drawings and all the rest. He was possessed by a sort of enormous hunger for painting.

He painted a huge number because he painted rapidly. And that is by no means an obvious truism.

By working quickly he reduces to nothing the margin for reflection between the canvas and himself. The weight of knowledge of art in his head and hand is such that its existence in Picasso is enough for him to be able to 'signify' more, the fewer signs he uses.

It is not automatic writing. For the conscious mind is standing guard, seeking the greatest possible reality in each movement, and cannot be swept aside for a moment. It is the very opposite of automatic writing (or writing which tries to be automatic). He is not seeking the truth of the subconscious which is repressed by thought. He is not seeking the pure, or impure, movement resulting from a mind swept clean.

On the contrary, he flings into the battle the immensity of his knowledge, his work and his astounding technique. They are there, armed and waiting, and he trusts to them when he attempts, by working at lightning speed, to leave a clear field for thought alone, the thought that demands to cleave to the painter and his model and show them as they are, without art interfering to add its own affectations.

Every time he shows a canvas in which a dot is enough for a breast, a dash for the painter, five spots of colour for a foot, a few pink or green stokes—there are a lot of pink and green canvases in this series of painters with their models—he says: '*That's enough, don't you think? What more do I need to do? What can I add to that? I've said it all . . .*'

*Picasso says ...*

If he stresses this point, it is not because he is trying to reduce to a minimum the colours and lines necessary to make a nude—or a painter—appear on the canvas. (Why should he want to do that? ...) In reality he knows that at such a speed he has time neither to conform to himself, Picasso, in his habits or what he believes to be his habits, nor to give in to certain 'modern' habits of which he says he wants to be rid at all cost.

By this means he seeks a truth that flashes forth, a spontaneous, natural way of expressing, in a single stroke, the reality at which he is aiming: the thing itself.

A young man came into my office and looked at the wall on which I had pinned, in order to see them more easily and all at once, or almost, some colour reproductions of Picasso's canvases. He looked at them all and said that the ones he liked best were 'the most finished things'. And that there were paintings there that were certainly very interesting, but struck him as rather too 'off-hand' to stand beside such masterpieces as, for instance, the 'Femmes au chat'.

I like 'off-hand' (even though it's quite the reverse). There is in fact a certain off-handedness in making a woman out of two crossed lines and ten little spots for nails at the ends. But this 'off-handedness' makes a woman—and that is the secret.

And what my young man called 'the finished canvases' are exactly the same. 'Finished' is a notion that has never had any meaning. Rembrandt was accused of producing canvases that were not finished. And you can light your cigarette at the 'finished' cigar stuck in the mouth of a Carolus Durand. 'Finished' or not is also an accepted notion we have to kill.

As far as that is concerned Picasso is in complete agreement with his time, with the most childishly self-confident and most noisily self-satisfied *avant-gardes* of his time. Apart from one exception, in which lies the immensity of his disagreement.

22

It is this. We must always kill accepted notions. But on condition that we do not kill painting at the same time.

Besides, the fact that Picasso aims in every canvas at the expression of the real person 'flashing' into paint, does not mean, naturally, that this is the only way he paints. Even while most strongly attracted by the laconicism of the pink and green canvases of the painters with models, he ranges far and wide at the same time. He paints more pictures of Jacqueline, more pictures of painters, large, very 'finished' portraits. He even mixes the two in the same painting. For example we see a painter (his head enormous and worked extremely elaborately in relief, with shadows and wrinkles, and swirls of beard and ears) looking out from the background of the canvas with great dreamy eyes, at a nude: that is to say a pink streak and black dots which are the eye, the nostrils, the navel, the sex-organs and the nails.

What reality they have for the painter looking at them! And what reality they both have for the painter who paints them both! . . .

And if we want to dig deeper and lose ourselves in the marvellous mazes of painters looking at models, also painted, in order to paint them, etc., etc. . . . we always come back to the painted painter looking with a view to capture, at a Picasso nude (a very 'off-hand' nude): reality.

It is for all this infinite complication of reality that he is seeking a living expression. Not one conforming to the modern demands of art, but one flowing directly from the source. Painting itself must take on a glowing new youth so that it may bring out essential truths with a single brush-stroke.

In other words if we must kill modern art it always amounts to saying that we must kill art itself.

Enough of art; we want life!

*Picasso says . . .*

What a strange thing is this painter obsessed with reality! All his life he has thought of nothing else, he has never parted from it, and yet he never invites it into his studio. He carries it around everywhere within himself. He looks at it within himself. Within himself he sees Jacqueline, and within himself he sees the painter.

Otherwise how could all these men have come to life outside him—all these men he has never seen and whom he knows so well?

We made their acquaintance in 1964, at midnight, one day at Notre-Dame de Vie. Picasso said '*There are still hundreds of drawings you don't know. You'll see. They're very funny*'.

They are men with cigarettes. They are holding them, putting them to their lips, puffing them. Or they haven't any. They are heads, sometimes with only a hand or an arm.

Everything Picasso has to say about them, the questions he asks, the expressions he gives them, are significant of a profound upheaval in the flesh of his work.

And in fact they are no ordinary heads. They are heads like the nudes.

They are men. First and foremost Picasso makes this clear: whoever they may be or wherever they may come from (many of them look like the gardener, or somebody) '*they have some truth about them*'.

He explains that all he would like is that people looking at them should not be looking at drawings '*but at gentlemen smoking cigarettes*'.

What he hopes he has achieved or will achieve, is that humanity should be so truly present in these drawings that they exist as people, not as lines of ink or paint.

They are men's heads, then. '*Like the ones you see in cafés*'. That one is gay. That one is preoccupied. That one is thoughtful and that one is not thinking of anything.

But all that is still literature '*just like what people always say when they look at drawings'*. We admit them into our own universe. We enlist them in our lives.

But those heads you simply can't. Their faces have a life of their own and their expressions a presence which puts them outside the painter's personal folklore, where all the beings he has created live and move.

They are not anonymous heads. They are heads like those on which, one after another, our glance rests when we are sitting in a café. We do not know them. But each has his own face, and we imagine that underneath it each has his own life, as we have ours.

Those heads are made to exist. When drawing them, Picasso aimed at a sort of human intensity, a man's weight, a man's expression. He sought to carry this image of man to the stage nearest to life. And to create, between the image and the man, *'an almost-confusion'*.

*'Having said that, one knows quite well what one means'*. he says. *'Of course it's absurd. But sometimes there's a head that's so true that you can have a relationship with it just as you can with a real one.'*

The portfolio of a hundred heads goes on producing its men with cigarettes. *'You have to do more, and more, and more'*. It's only by doing more and more that you get anywhere; Picasso always says that.

Here, by doing more and more, by trying to make of each of these heads *'someone who exists'* he has completely emancipated their features.

Before, in whatever way he drew them, his heads had two eyes, a nose and a mouth.

Today they are heads, with nothing missing, and yet, in order to draw heads, there is absolutely no need to mark out their attributes one by one.

He draws these heads in the same way as he draws his painters and his nudes.

In them, he aims at a flashing out of head, a straight left of head, smashing into the canvas. He projects himself in a straight left to the canvas or the drawing.

Or else they are the same as they always are.

Or else streaks of paint whose direction is not determined by the need for a nose as such, or a mouth as such, *make* the face with apparent off-handedness, pregnant with infinite knowledge. For the face is there. All it needs is a spectator, and it is there.

And yet these complicated quadrilles of red, green and yellow streaks or spots, following no known trail, make a head.

Drawing his head, seeking to make it as immediate, as human, as he can—and precisely because it is the weight of humanity he wants to achieve, in defiance of all 'art'—he spreads the wings of his painting wider still. In order to reach man as he is, he even takes away from him his sacrosanct features; he replaces them with features of his own invention which give man a face-in-painting, as true as the other, and yet completely independent of the other. Even if they are the same.

Picasso says: *If I stick three pieces of wood on to a board and call it a painting, that isn't freedom; how could that possibly be freedom? It's doing something or other with three pieces of wood . . . It has nothing to do with freedom.*

*If there is freedom in what one does, it's the fact of liberating something within oneself. And even that doesn't last.*

And now the studio with the 'off-hand' painters and models is suddenly full of canvases of heads which are more off-hand than ever. But what a weight of off-handedness! It gushes forth on all sides. All the studios are full of it. Concentric rows of heads look at us.

Look at us is the word. For they all have looks of great concentration, their eyes press heavily on us. Picasso's painting

26

has always had a look. But never so much as in these heads
that are made for that.

For they have to exist.

That is what he is seeking. That is what he says. And it is
no accident that he mixes with the Heads the little canvases
in which painters and models are summed up in those few
streaks and spots I was talking about. The painters and the
nudes have heads like the Heads, they are made like them altogether. Green crosses and pink snakes give them a face,
and they look out on the world from all their circles that are
eyes.

Picasso stresses the fact that above all he would like these
Heads to be '*someone*'.

He emphasises the personality of each.

Suddenly he declares that besides, with all those heads you
could do anything you liked.

You could even make a Last Supper.

Immediately the studio becomes a field for picking apostles
in. According to Saint John and according to Saint Matthew.
In these heads lie mysteries which are also certainties. They
are someone if you want them to be. No other Saint Thomas
is possible, no other Saint Peter hearing the cock crow. Only
Judas is difficult. Picasso tells why.

Because instinctively we all turn towards the 'distorted'
head, the head whose disordered features are in wicked contrast with those which are not 'determined' and which the
mind invents, while watching the colours dance on their faces
as in a public square.

'*One looks for a modern Judas*', says Picasso. '*There you
see what I mean . . .*'

We have great trouble finding Christ. But we finally agree
on a Head. This one too looks like the gardener.

That is how Picasso works.

We cannot say, as the custom is nowadays, that he is
coming back to representational art; he never left it.

His own, of course.

*Picasso says* . . .

But we can say that at a point in the history of painting when it is said to be being rehumanized, but unfortunately by methods outside painting, Picasso is trying to increase tenfold the real humanity of his creations, but by methods which increase tenfold the power of painting.

# Picasso says . . .

## NAMING THINGS

Picasso had just been showing us serious faces with huge close-set eyes, sort of Mona Lisas with elongated hands, a multiplication of women seated in their dresses with the Afghan hound Kaboul close against the folds of their skirts, women engrossed beneath hats, or bareheaded with eyes and hair in every shape and position; one with a little head, full face and double profile, within her great sombre profile, one whose hand rests on her cheek and whose eyes are enormous, one with piled-up tiers of chignons and glances, one whose eyes are like the flowers in her hat. Their fingers, their breasts, their eyes, their legs, their shoes with their heels and their hair with their ribbons, their sleeves, their lips on all sides, and the formidable weight of their presence and their gaze.

They are the Dames de Mougins, the queens, the beloved ones, the Jacquelines, all watching us at once with an incomparable serenity. From time to time Picasso rises, walks up to the canvases, picks up a dozen, takes them away, stacks them against a wall, and, one after another, brings a new batch.

Then he goes and sits down again, and silence takes shape once more in the presence of this fresh assembly of women before us. We examine them with such force and intensity that I feel we are about to become like them as we plunge our eyes, so solemnly questioning, deep into their eyes, their lips, the ribbons in their hair.

*Picasso says . . .*

We were looking at a few slender strokes, close together in a great empty space, which were sufficient in themselves to make the two arms, and two hands with their ten fingers, the strength of their clasp, the weight of the hands on the knees, their shape, everything. Picasso said:

*What we have to do is to NAME things. They have to be called by their names. I NAME an eye. I NAME a foot. I NAME my dog's head on my knees. I NAME my knees . . . NAMING—that's all. That's enough.*

He added '*I don't know whether I make myself really clear when I talk about naming. I mean giving a name. Remember Eluard's poem. Liberty. "To name you, Liberty".*

*. . . I am born to know you*
*To name you*
*Liberty . . .*
*He named it. That's what you must do.*'

## SOMETHING SACRED

Picasso speaks of painting time and time again, but he never writes about it. Writing fixes an idea, but speech leaves it free to be or not to be at the same time. Picasso never betrays a painting idea by flinging it into the eternity of words. Who has not tried to wrest from him replies to all the questions men ask him? He never writes them down. And thus he has never given the appearance of a formula to a single one of the thoughts with which he overflows at every instant. They change ceaselessly, like his painting. Truth can at any moment become its opposite.

One day he simply jotted down on the last page of a notebook: '*Painting is stronger than I am. It makes me do what it wants.*'

As soon as the canvas is begun, at the first stroke of the

brush, the painter loses his freedom. He tries to impose his will. He works hard at it. But painting is there, and there is nothing to be done against it . . . That is the fate of painters. They are entirely of its opinion. It is within them and outside of them at the same time.

It is a strange trade, a strange destiny, if you think about it. Putting paint on canvas and slaving, persisting, torturing oneself, struggling, fighting oneself, the canvas, the whole world, working day and night, and then what?

'Why? What forces us to do it?' says Picasso. 'Ah! No one can know what it is! . . .'

That is a familiar saying of his. Meaning that those who have not been through it cannot have any idea of what sort of a trade it is.

That is why, above everything and perhaps next after poets, it is painters he loves the most.

All painters. They are legion. They have no name and every name. They are bad and they are good. They have genius; genius, transcendent or banal. But they are all painters, they are all brothers. The simple fact of choosing, rightly or wrongly, this crazy trade, weaves a bond between them, whoever they are. They know 'what it is'. They alone can understand, even if what they paint has little or no merit, provided that it is done in honesty and not in guile. They are knights of the same order, sitting before the world from eternity to eternity, and wondering why . . .

And so we talked. If, he said, we could find out how it is that one canvas suddenly has something and another hasn't, there would be no more problems of creation: all we would have to do would be to manufacture successful canvases.

(Horrible thought. But what peace of mind! Mr. So-and-so, masterpiece maker. Formula established by centuries of experience. Painters of masterpieces, from father to son since the Pieta of Avignon and the bison . . .)

But why is it that suddenly there comes into the world, into a studio, one, two or ten canvases in which something has been born and gone on living? (And what, anyway?)

31

About which we feel as we look at them that they are above and beyond everything that has ever been achieved. That something more has entered into them. That from all this work this head has been born, at which we have only to look in order to feel its distance and its power, its existence, its fabulous participation in the world from which it springs forth by so simple a means, and whose consecrated witness it becomes.

'Something sacred, that's it,' says Picasso. 'We ought to be able to say that word, or something like it, but people would take it the wrong way, and give it a meaning it hasn't got. We ought to be able to say that such and such a painting is as it is, with its capacity for power, because it is 'touched by God'. But people would put a wrong interpretation on it. And yet it's the nearest we can get to the truth . . .'

There's no explanation we can give in words. Unless it is that, through a relationship of creative man with all that is highest in the human spirit, something happens which gives painted reality this power.

'You can search for a thousand years,' he says, 'and you'll find nothing.' Today everything can be explained scientifically. Except that. We can go to the moon and walk on the bottom of the sea—anything; but painting remains painting because it escapes these investigations. It stays there like a question; and only it can give the answer.

In that it is lucky. And unlucky. And so are we.

PLAYING

One of the most common ways of betraying Picasso is to believe, or let oneself believe, or pretend to believe, that in all this he is PLAYING at painting.

His 'craft' is so fabulous in every way that he can do

anything. So they say. And so he plays. With Delacroix, with Velasquez or Manet. With himself. He takes a theme and plays with it. The reality is the exact opposite.

His 'craft' is so fabulous in every way that it gives him a sort of painter's licence.

And it is within this 'painter's licence' that he is passionately in quest of another freedom.

## WORK

*'If you know exactly what you are going to do'* says Picasso, *'what's the good of doing it? There's no interest in something you know already. It's much better to do something else.'*

## PAINTING OUT OF DOORS

How wonderful nature is—it can even serve as a studio. Sometimes Picasso brings canvases out on to the gravel, and suddenly we have a private view in the garden, with canvases leaning quite naturally against trees or windows, and the daylight envelops them and never plays them false; you would think they were breathing in the naturalness of their pose, unframed and unhung, the canvas itself becoming a natural presence in natural surroundings.

The last time I saw them in the open, the canvases were those of the 'Déjeuner sur l'Herbe', and nothing in the world could have suited them better than that silent out-ofdoors where the canvases swarm in an atmosphere with which they themselves were already filled.

33

## EYES

Jacqueline's eyes, huge and black, converge on me from all sides. They appear in cut-out figures, they are shaped like fish or magic candles, they are the same and side by side, they are both there in the profile, looking at me, or each on the iron surface of a face, they fly across the sheets of paper pinned to the walls, they take every place and every position, they are one below the other, one above the other, perpendicularly; they turn their backs on each other, encircle the head, move head downwards, form a circumspect row beneath a hat, bristle beneath a ribbon, they are black, huge and of every colour, and their lashes dance around them like the rays of the sun, and with the same freedom.

## THE LINE

A discussion carried on in front of the Indian ink drawings. Picasso shows us the spots and explains how, not limited by lines, but spots, as they are, they alone can evoke, express and bring into being the true line.

Then he shows us pencil drawings and says they are the only ones that exist, basically, because they give the only possible line in a thousand . . .

'Possible for me at that particular moment', he says.

## GARGANTUA

The sum of work accomplished by Picasso in these last few years goes beyond the liveliest imagination. He seems to work more and more as time goes on. You leave him and disappear for a month, then you come back and there may be fifty new canvases at least, not counting all the other things in the studios. Apart from the summer when people, sun, sea and the pull of the beach break the diabolical rhythm, the fire burns without remission. Canvases are sent for in a tearing hurry. There aren't enough. Jacqueline has to go and fetch some from Cannes. And again. Sometimes three times in one day. The shop-keeper opens his eyes wide, as though faced with an anxious mother unable to satisfy her Gargantuan child.

And all this doesn't take into account the pictures beneath pictures. You go away leaving twenty painters in their studio. When you come back there are twenty more, but half the first lot are missing—they're underneath the new ones. And there have been dozens in the interval. I'm not talking about a picture in the course of being painted, but of pictures finished, begun again, finished again, piled one on the other until only one is left, no thicker for all its secrets.

In this cataract of painting that swells from year to year, there is a flow of ideas which reaches out to the onlooker and sweeps him along. He is surrounded by the swarming activity of creation. The incomparable knowledge of his art which gives Picasso his dazzling supremacy monopolises all possible means of expression and discovery. Picasso fights, and it is always he who has the choice of weapons, and he chooses all of them and wins, and he wonders constantly whether he hasn't lost, and he begins again. And the jungle of creation lies all around, wild and full of orchids, and fruits of war and love and single-mindedness. The jungle of the studio.

## RAPHAEL

'If Raphael', says Picasso, 'came back now, with exactly the
same canvases, nobody would buy a single one from him.
Nobody would even look at him.'

## FÉNÉON AND THE DEMOISELLES

Picasso relates that one day Fénéon came to see him, brought
by somebody or other, at the Bateau-Lavoir in the Rue Ravig-
non, where he received him in company with the Demoiselles
d'Avignon. Fénéon said to Picasso: 'You ought to do carica-
tures.'

'And yet Fénéon was quite somebody', says Picasso.

## GOOD WILL TO ALL MEN

'The terrible thing nowadays', says Picasso, 'is that nobody
speaks ill of anybody. If we believe all we read, all's well. In
every exhibition there's something. And in any case, everything goes, or nearly everything. They can be indifferent or
even a little spiteful. But nobody slaughters anybody, one
thing's as good as another, you don't wipe the floor with anything, or crack anything up to the skies. Everything's on one
level. Why? Surely not because it's true. Well, then? Because
they aren't thinking any more? Or because they daren't say
what they think?'

## HOMAGE TO VAN GOGH

Picasso talks about Van Gogh all the time, and thinks about him all the time; he often contrasts him, not without bitterness, with the spoilt, self-satisfied arrogance of the times we are living through in painting. For him, Van Gogh is the one painter whose life was exemplary, up to and including his death.

## THE PRESENCE

Picasso's life magnetises the things and people around him. His way of life, his way of being at home, in painting and in society, conditions and transforms all his surroundings. He charges all accumulators, whether of objects or animals. Though he has the gift of giving to the works around him (his and those of others) a life of their own, though he makes them live with all the thoughts he is constantly bestowing upon them, though he finally gives them a share in daily life by living intertwined with them, living only through them and for them, he does not express his relationship with them as one of either creator or master. From the moment when he does them, their existence begins, and they are what they are, placed around him like question marks. That, too, is what makes the enchantment of this house where the pottery owl and the portrait of Jacqueline play their part in the drama of everyday life, in a way absolutely different from that of canvases shackled to the walls of art galleries.

## NEVER WITHOUT ITS OPPOSITE

The most often-quoted saying of Picasso is this:
*'I do not seek. I find.'*
It is wonderfully bold and sure, but can only be explained, if he really said it, by constant reference to its opposite.
*'One never stops searching because one never finds.'*
In reality he finds constantly and seeks constantly. He has scarcely finished a canvas when he looks at it in search of the secrets he has himself just put into it. And he begins another. which takes him where he does not want to go when he takes it where it does not want to go. And so on . . .

## ONE STYLE FOR EACH

Picasso explains that a certain way of drawing is an anomaly.
In order that the drawing may be true, according to his present ideas, the method of approach has to be completely changed.
For *example*, he says (speaking to a painter), *when you do a head you have to draw like that head. Ingres drew like Ingres, and not like the things he was drawing. If for example you take a tree. At the foot of the tree there is a goat, and beside the goat a little girl looking after the goat. Well, you need a different style for each. The goat is round, the little girl is square, the tree is a tree.*
*And yet people use the same style of drawing for all three. It's that that's wrong. Each one needs a completely different style of drawing.*

## THE LOUVRE AND DUFAYEL

Picasso says that today it isn't painting that's required; it's art. People want art. He adds:

*You must be able to be vulgar.*

*When we were with Braque, we said: 'There's the Louvre, and there's Dufayel.' And we judged everything like that. That was our way of judging the paintings we looked at.*

*We said: 'Oh no, that's the Louvre again.'*

*But there, there, is just a little Dufayel! . . .*

## MOVEMENT

*For me the role of painting, says Picasso, is not to depict movement, to show reality in movement. Its role, for me, is rather to halt movement.*

*You must go further than movement in order to halt an image.*

*Otherwise you're chasing after it.*

*For me, only at that moment is there reality.*

## DAUBS

Picasso says, as he shows us someone's painting:

*What interests me about this daub is that it comes out as horses.*

*Otherwise I could do a thousand daubs and they'd always be the same.*

39

*Picasso says . . .*

He adds:

*One has the impression that everyone is horribly afraid of reality. If there's the tiniest bit of it people are horrified and get rid of it.*

## PAINTERS

Picasso is often heard to say that when he paints, all the painters are with him in the studio. Or rather behind him. Watching him.

Those of yesterday, and those of today.

Velasquez never left him during the time when he was painting Las Meninas. Delacroix was constantly watching over him while he did the Femmes d'Alger.

And he wondered what Delacroix was thinking. Whether he was pleased. Or displeased.

And all the other painters were there too, those we know and those we don't, those whose catalogues are sent to us, the young, the unknown, the famous, all of them. Their presence of painting itself, of both yesterday and today.

And of its million problems.

Problems which, as with all painters, go round and round in Picasso's head, coming face to face with his own.

A painter in solitude is never alone.

## LOOK OUT FOR THE LUNATIC!

I settle myself in the upper studio, with the Heads. The air is burning with a mad blaze of sunshine although the season for the beaches is ending. The vast panorama of the window-panes all the length of the house has the transparent beauty of September. I gaze at the canvases propped one against the other. I gaze and I gaze. I imagine I am thinking, but in reality I am just gazing; it is the same thing, only more difficult. This goes on for quite a while. Picasso sticks his head through the little window of the bathroom which opens into the studio, like that of the bedroom, which gives a puppet-show appearance to this half-body appearing in the wall. He thrusts his head through and yells at me: *'Look out for the lunatic!'*

## IF ONE WAS A PAINTER . . .

Blessed painting, queen of all time! For a true painter, painting isn't somebody painting all day, nor café-diplomacy, nor eternal chatter about 'what is painting?' or 'why do you paint?', or other subjects of conversation with which this century loves to feed its obtuseness and its emptiness.

For the true painter, the painting for which he is the vehicle transforms time to a question. To do or not to do? And why do or not do? This, or that? One ought to paint everything, embrace everything, try everything, open the whole earth to one's understanding.

Picasso has a passion for reality that would devour everything if it could. The whole vast world presses to join in his desire. Everything, he feels, should lend itself to his need, and become painting.

When he is not painting, he always seems, nevertheless, to be painting all the time. In any case he looks intensely; that is his way of painting when he is not in his studio. And in his moments of relaxation, or at least of silence and immobility,

41

he looks at the world as he looks at his painting in the studio, with the same anxious questioning.

He often repeats, rather mockingly, a saying which means very exactly what it means. . . . If he sees a pretty girl lying, all curves, on the beach, or a fine fat huge giantess tottering under the weight of her full-blown bulk (and actually far more often the giantess than the pretty girl) or a prodigious belly, or a head that doesn't look like one, he says:

'*What a pity one isn't a painter! If one was a painter one could do her portrait!*'

The painter of the 'Painter and his model', the one who works on Picasso's canvases in the studio, would never hesitate to do everything. Picasso says that with a sigh, but in the manner of the lady in the dining-room showing a bunch of flowers to her guests. 'Ah! if one was a painter! . . .' she says.

Picasso to a painter:

'*You who are a painter, what is stopping you from painting her portait? You're so lucky,*' Laughing, a little envious, as though he were an architect.

In reality he thinks and says that everything ought to be painted. Outside the studio, all that part of the world (almost the whole world) that his painting leaves aside of necessity, torments him. A thousand times a day, outside or inside, he says: '*It's magnificent. And yet I'm painting everything except that. One ought to paint everything.*'

He paints more than anyone in the world. But it's what he doesn't paint that tempts him. He still has, for example, to paint: the world, minus the warriors, at the moment when he is painting them. It is a great deal. This choice, a tiny one when all is said and done, makes the unexplored universe even more monstrously huge than it really is.

There were five or six of us, including Picasso and Jacqueline, eating together on the Croisette, on the terrace of a

Cannes restaurant. It was the end of summer, and the kind of night into which one longs to plunge as though into a sea. But on the pavement in front of us, in the bright light of the café terraces, a lively, mysterious crowd, the crowd of Cannes, swarmed in both directions. We were fascinated.

Girls in shorts a few inches long, showing interminable legs, beautiful as the day, or on the other hand without the figure for that sort of thing, rubbing shoulders with extravagant dowagers decked out in sheath dresses, sequins and foundation cream, with summer-beaten necks sweating under sable or mink stoles; narrow-shouldered melancholy-faced American sailors, their white trousers drawn tightly over their buttocks, mechanically chewing gum; young dreamboats in casual gear, with hard or melting eyes, old men clamped in their white suits on the seats of their Jaguars, and made to be packed away at night into a drawer, piece by piece, like 'the general of whom nothing was left'; mothers with their babies, and families taking the air, dragging each other by the hand; a girl to dream of, a girl to kill, a girl to weep for, and so on . . .

Fascinated, we watched the stream, terrifyingly, marvellously renewed from second to second.

*One ought to paint all that, said Picasso. But how? How could one really manage to paint all that AS IT IS, not forgetting the lady's little dog and the squinting sailor? All at once, exactly as we see them there. And us as well, since we are there too. But how could it be done? It's impossible . . .*

And anyway, how could you do it in writing? That can't be done either.


The question is often asked but never answered.

Ah, how lucky the eye is to grasp it all so swiftly!

In the time it takes for 'the written word' to count up the dowager's jewels, the sailors from the aircraft-carrier or the fisherman's children, ten thousand others will have passed.

Well then, a single line of poetry. For one soldier is enough for a battle.

But that is another matter.

A camera, then?

That is another matter. Something fixed.

Then the cinema.

That is perhaps what would come nearest, and at the same time would be the most likely to give a false idea. For with all this sweetness of the summer night, the thoughts which this crowd suggests to us (and which the written word can tell where the crowd cannot), this face that stands out (and which a photograph can crystallize) the cinema can only record its flow as it is. Without us.

Extraordinary, but—without us. With the genius of a producer making his crowd conform to the ideas it inspires in him. But then it won't be the same crowd. Nor the same ideas ... And in any case, as Picasso says, the people looking on *'will be somewhere else, they won't be us looking on. They will be outside'.*

The discussion, or rather the desultory conversation, the quiet delirium, went on like this, while the crowd continued to cock a snook at the ideas we shot at them from all angles. Picasso argued passionately.

Was there, then, nothing left but painting, that major art? The only one perhaps, capable of truly recreating, on a terrible, motionless plane, the eye's reality, but charged throughout with intelligence, plus the reality of light and night and our thoughts and all the movement around? And would it all be invented?

*'And all the same, and all different'*, said Picasso.

The crowd continued to pass, unaware that it was an impregnable citadel.

*'And yet,'* said Picasso, *'if one was a painter!'*

When he painted at Vallauris 'The little girl skipping', he first painted a canvas. In it the ground is marked by a little stroke.

Or rather, shadow.

Not long ago he received, cast in bronze, the sculpture

which he made of the same picture, and which is at Notre-
Dame de Vie.

At the time when he was creating it from its elements, it
was the sculpture which needed the greatest research into
reality. The problem of the little girl in mid-air did not trouble
the painter.

But the sculptor had to get out of the difficulty. How? One
day Picasso appeared radiantly happy. He had just been working on the problem in space of the little girl skipping. *'I've
discovered'*, he said, *'what the little girl is resting on when she
is in mid-air. On the rope, naturally! Why hadn't I thought of
it? . . . I only had to look at reality . . .'*

Reality, reality, reality. . . . We talk about it so much that
you might think it didn't exist, or that its existence was
really important, since we have to keep on hammering at it
in order to think of it at all.

And yet so many paintings make appeal to it. . . . All, in
fact. Since they say inner reality can stand aside from reality
in general, and be none the less reality for that.

When we speak of Picasso's work, we cannot help speaking
of his reality, his Golden Fleece, his Holy Grail.

He said one day: *Reality is a word you find everywhere.
It's mixed into every sauce. But the odd thing is that there's
nothing ever made that doesn't claim to derive from it.*

*'From the most conventional to the most conventional, and
from the most modern to the most modern—or supposed to be
modern—it's reality. It's funny. Even when people say they've
succeeded in doing without it . . .'*

On April 5, 1960, he painted a little jet-black picador,
and a little jet-black bull, making the jet-black horse rear up
in front of a little jet-black torero waving his cape. They are
all alone in the arena which turns and turns back on itself like
a snail-shell, with a wide sky above and around, and those vast
numbers of dots on the tiers of seats (without seats) which are
the crowd.

45

*Picasso says . . .*

This is the corrida. The little scene of the picador, the mata-dor and the bull occupies the attention, and the arena occupies the space.

'*What I would like*', says Picasso, '*is to do a corrida as it really is.*'

Someone replies that every time he paints a bull, a ban-derillero, a crowd, a horse, it is the corrida as it really is, isn't it? Even at the bottom of a little earthenware cup or a large dish.

'*I would like to do it as I see it*', says Picasso.

But isn't that the way he sees it? When he does it? Isn't that the way Goya did his bullfights, by seeing them? Picasso says:

'*Yes, but that isn't the whole corrida. I should like to do it with everything, the whole of the arena, the whole of the crowd, the whole of the sky, the bull as it is and the bull-fighter too, the whole cuadrilla, the banderilleros and the music and the man selling paper hats . . .*' A REAL corrida.

Obviously the bull would have to be done life-size (he has actually done this). But then what about the arena all round it?

'*You'd need a canvas as big as the arena . . . it's appalling not to be able to do it; it would be magnificent . . .*'

And when you come down to it, what's stopping him? 'The Marriage at Cana' is big, somebody says. Picasso says that beside the arena, 'The Marriage at Cana' is tiny.

He ponders, and finally suggests the simplest of solutions: a canvas as cumbersome as that would have to be done in the arena. It would be completely round, and would naturally be the shape of an arena . . . And not a real bull? 'One Sunday at Nimes', says Jacqueline, 'and we'd be sitting in the front row.' 'Oh well', says Picasso, 'it's only a joke. But I've been thinking about that canvas for a long time, and there's noth-ing to say that one day I won't find a way of doing it.'

## PICASSO THE MORALIST

Nobody can say that Picasso has not suffered enough with the world.

He suffers, he grows angry, he hits back, he commits himself. He never fails to take sides.

And yet every time he enters the struggle he suffers more. All the contradictions of the age leap to strike him. Dreadful wounds appear, in his enthusiasm, his generosity, his work, and his glory. But he is Saint George and the Dragon at one and the same time, and all his heads repel the attack.

He is an iron warrior, an iron man, an iron painter. And yet everything wounds him, everything weighs on him, and over and over again he is sick with disgust at seeing something that seemed so clear and simple foundering in all the pros and cons of mediocrity.

Why should Picasso, shut up in his studio, not be peacefully happy in the perpetual unhappiness of painting, which is his job?

Why should he have to live other lives than his own, with its hours choked with an infinity of problems, and all that crushing lack of time that is his only incurable wound?

What impels him to hurl himself into ten thousand battles where he is so often slain, even if he gains the victory?

After all he could be, for himself, a very suitable and sufficient centre of the universe.

But there is in Picasso a strange virtue, a tremendous stubbornness that refuses to suffer injustice, revolts against any attempt at violence, and makes war against war or on the side of the warrior, against prison or on the side of liberty for men and ideas.

He exalts the hero and detests slaughter.

Willy-nilly, in spite of himself, spontaneously or taking himself firmly in hand, he paints a manifesto whenever the age he lives in urges him to it by some senseless act.

Then he becomes accuser and judge.

47

He thunders against the inevitable end, of blows blindly struck, of murderous stupidity. On a higher plane, against ignorance, stupidity, cowardice.

On the highest plane of all he come to grips with death itself.

He is the fiery champion of man massacred by man in all the Guernicas on earth, and of man preyed upon unjustly by that one invulnerable warrior: death.

Mougins, winter 1963–64.

At Mougins, winter out of doors has its famous sun, but the nights in the studio are more magnificent still, warm, intimate, and deep.

I have a memory, extraordinarily violent and almost magical in its clarity, of an evening that winter at Notre-Dame de Vie, before Christmas. At the end of the room Picasso generally uses when he is not working, there is a studio which he had built on a terrace. The wall facing the vast countryside (with its motorway at the foot of the hill and its sea studded with the shining triangles of warships) is glass for half its height. The whole of the night lives in this window with its strings of lights, its sparks flashing from earth and sky, the one alive with the red and white meteor-streaks of cars, and the other fixed and motionless, with no shooting stars. These vastnesses of the night, so precious to the eye, so inviting to the dreams of the man behind the glass, are both outside and inside at the same time.

Around us was the still fairly calm disorder of the studio, for at that time Picasso was only just beginning really to use it.

The farthest wall was uncluttered, vast and white. This wall had a part to play.

It all began late in the evening when Picasso came out of his studio at the far end and walked towards us. The lights went out. Jacqueline raised a finger, and a jet of light sprang forth. And suddenly there appeared, enormous, ten times larger than the real canvas and covering the whole wall, in colours, a bare-legged warrior, his foot planted on a child, beside a kneeling woman, clinging to him, her head thrown back, screaming; it was Poussin's 'Massacre of the Innocents'.

All around, right to the farthest corners of the wall, the massacre went on. There was no house left, no studio, nobody. Only those huge people radiating colour and light, alone in the night, on a level with the house, and with an extraordinary life of their own.

But the dark landscape clung to the glass, making it into a mirror. Another 'Massacre of the Innocents' appeared before our eyes, right opposite the first.

'*It's almost better than the other*', said Picasso, '*because it's less sharp, and the colours are truer.*'

Floating as it did outside the wall, in the air, covering, by the usual optical illusion, the whole sky, with its stars which took their place in the canvas, with the whole of the hill of Mougins, and a few eyes that were headlights gliding among the soldiers as they raised their sabres, the 'Massacre of the Innocents' on the glass wall had a feeling of singular immensity.

In the studio where we sat invisible, where all was dark, thoughts of all kinds grew in profusion, and from time to time were expressed aloud, facelessly. It was not the first time the miracle of the projector and the size of that wall had transformed that studio into an enchanted art gallery where all the galleries in the world showed us the many-times-magnified essence of their masterpieces. 'La ronde de nuit' here appears life-size. A head by Rembrandt, ten feet high, can be contemplated for hours, whether true or false, with all sorts of details suddenly becoming clear as though under a microscope. The head of Van Gogh's self-portrait stretches from floor to ceiling. And even though it is the Van Gogh pictures which suffer most from reproduction, Picasso says that all the same, on the wall as everywhere else, it is he who is the greatest of all.

But this 'Massacre of the Innocents' was a surprise. For Picasso appeared yet again as the prey of a fixed idea, an obsession, a theme eclipsing all else. Once more he was the captive of his own demands, tied to the development of the canvases he had begun. He had just entered on the period which was to be known as 'The rape of the Sabine women'.

And perhaps never, since 'Las Meninas', had he devoted himself to his work with such passion and such suffering.

Why warriors?

It is a theme, the world over, strange in its magnificence and its cruelty.

A massacre must be painted if it is to be denounced. The warriors have heads of stone. Their gestures are ferocious. And, at the same time, magnificent. They are evil, and for that very reason all-powerful. They are death, and death itself must appear under their skin and their helmets, and under the hoofs and teeth of their horses.

In the theme of war and slaughter there exists, inexorably, this dialectic of pity and death, of violence and cruelty, of beauty to the point of madness, and blood to the normal point of unbearableness which is the essence of the corrida. For the matador and for the bull. Always on the side of the man who is threatened. But always on the side of the fighting bull. Relieved by the death of the bull. And at the same time saluting the bull. Always torn between the thousand contradictory knife-thrusts of life and death in the arena, where feeling is never wholly what it is, always mingled with fear or pain on one side or the other, admiration or horror, enthusiasm or terror; where feeling never banishes that terrible restless wave of thoughts which accompanies every movement in the arena and which presents, again and again, all bleeding, the problems of life, death, grandeur, courage, injustice and heroism.

That winter, Picasso wanted to paint warriors. The origin of this decision, or rather the catalyst of the idea, was a project of the Salon de Mai which suggested to its exhibitors—of whom Picasso is one—a theme inspired by Delacroix: for example 'The entry of the Crusaders into Constantinople'. In other words, in the spirit of Delacroix, the victor in presence of the slaughtered innocents.

Pignon passed this suggestion on to Picasso, who accepted with enthusiasm.

Picasso pondered on this theme.

There he found himself on the same level as his brother-painters, a thing he loves more than anything.

His brother-painters, moreover, seized the opportunity to spring at each other's throats with the utmost violence. These, however, were the ones who habitually exhibited at this Salon. They talked about a scandalous return to subject painting. 'As for that', said Picasso, 'I've never been afraid of subjects.' (These words are taken from a telephone conversation with Pignon who was telling him about the dramas going on in Paris). 'I've been given a commission and I'm getting on with it. You can take fifty thousand pictures, abstract ones, or anything of that sort, or tachist, even if the canvas is green, well, the subject is green. There's always a subject.

'It's rubbish to think of cutting out the subject, it's impossible. It's as if you said: "pretend I'm not there." You just try it.'

And later, at Notre-Dame de Vie, he took the other side, as usual: 'A warrior, naturally, if he has no helmet and no horse and no head, he's much easier to do. But for my part, at that point he simply doesn't interest me. At that point he might just as well be a chap getting on to a train. What interests me in a warrior is the warrior.'

So that winter he talked of nothing but his warriors. He said terrible things were going on in his studio from every point of view. 'It's never been like this', he said, 'It's the most difficult thing I've ever done.'

It was not the first time he had said that. The birth of any painting is painful, and some series in this domain have lacerated the painter on their way into the world. For example 'Las Meninas'.

He often adds: 'I don't know how much good that is, it's possibly appalling. But in any case I'm doing it, I'm doing thousands of it.'

51

What were these warriors? We only knew that Picasso was utterly absorbed in his work.

One day he said:

'*That's not Delacroix at all. It's wavering between Poussin and David. But it hasn't any connection. Perhaps it's the Innocents, and perhaps it's the Sabine women. . . .*'

After all this he asked to be sent, if possible, reproductions of Poussin and of the Sabine women.

On the same occasion he did not neglect to ask whether the painters of the Salon de Mai would allow his slight deviation from Delacroix to Poussin or David or both.

Whether it mattered or not. He considers himself in this Salon as a painter invited on the same terms as the others. He wants no exception to be made.

He appeared very pleased and reassured to be told that many painters had done the same thing, from Memlinc to Seurat, or hadn't taken a theme at all. He didn't understand why, though. He said he would have considered the idea a magnificent one, if only he hadn't felt the need to carry it out, which, he declared, had plunged him into unimaginable distress.

There are quite a number of painters who like to come to grips with a subject at a time when it is really no longer common practice. Despite the trouble and difficulties, Picasso still feels a certain exaltation at the idea. He is a painter who likes painters and likes to participate. In everything. Particularly when it is difficult.

That is why, on the evening of which I was speaking, we gave him a surprise by preparing everything in the studio, the projector and the chairs, for the show. And that is how, when he left his work with his warriors, to whom he had returned as soon as dinner was over, he suddenly found himself in the presence of the 'Massacre' on the wall and the 'Massacre' on the window.

In reality this story of the 'Entry of the Crusaders into Constantinople' and of Delacroix changing into Poussin and David and finishing up as Picasso is a mere anecdote.

Picasso has the theme of the 'Massacre of the Innocents' in his blood. No theme in a thousand forms is more familiar to him. His adherence to this idea, its service to him, all the canvases and drawings he derives from it, stem from a quality he has within him, a quality not particularly widespread in this century, and so often questioned in the realms of creation: the gift of participation.

In reality, Good and Evil in a thousand familiar guises haunt his work, and his thought is that of a moralist who, every time the need has arisen, has emphasised in painting— and clearly—Good, Evil and the direction which must be followed if the one is to triumph over the other. He paints the morals of his time.

This portrait, severe as it is, is entirely true. There is in Picasso an inflexible human morality. If we were to gather together everything in his work which denounces violence, celebrates freedom and peace, rejects war, utters a rallying-cry to the help of the innocent, and sings the praises of the hero; if we were to follow the hundreds and thousands of canvases and drawings which point the way through his work by his participation in the battles of his time, we would see that they comprise by themselves a complete moral science of our time.

When I write of Picasso, that master of irony and hard-hitting repartee, whose speech flows endlessly in terrible patterns of words and ideas or explodes with a power and pitch far beyond the normal—the man who, respecting nothing, respects everything, whose words and thoughts are at the service of a perfect liberty in which morality plays no part, nor modesty, nor opportunity, who can kill with a word, and with a word knows how to lift his companion into the seventh heaven, this man of such rare intelligence, with intelligent hands holding the accumulated knowledge of every known civilization, I do not hesitate to write these words of him: 'Picasso the moralist'.

And yet, at the very moment when I am writing them, my-self sharing of necessity in this atmosphere so utterly impregnated with his spirit and his thought-habits, where those who approach him do so at their own risk or to their supreme delight, at the very moment when I am thinking, over and over, of 'Picasso the moralist', so certain of expressing a basic truth which is in no way out of the ordinary—and I don't know myself why I fasten on to it with such satisfaction, as though it were a great discovery—I catch myself smiling with pleasure. Knowing that at the very moment when you have just decided that Picasso has been defined, all truth collapses if you refuse to see in him a truth which appears the exact opposite.

He is a reluctant moralist, for this attitude sets him the worst of problems. Knowing this he never hesitates to adopt it.

It is natural to him, he could not exist otherwise. He knows it and suffers from it, but he finds it hard to become resigned to himself. He could kill himself, for example, in his fury at having begun these warriors, which are pure self-torture. He is also a moralist whose mind is quite free from fetters (even those fetters which are called moral), who mocks himself, kills with a word what he adores, laughs at the worst that can happen, and will not allow any intelligence or any interest to anyone he meets whose mind is closed to the absolute necessity of absolute liberty in everything.

But he takes nothing lightly, he takes everything seriously. He is, then, a moralist who does not admit what is generally called morality.

Moralists like him are the only true ones.

And if I smile as I write these lines, it is because I am still recalling that evening with the Poussin warrior in duplicate. Don't imagine it was a serene and religious contemplation. We sat in darkness as we faced the luminous warrior, and we attacked him—and Poussin at the same time—desultorily, incoherently, with the same conviction with which, a second later, we heaped praises on them both.

In Picasso's thoughts this was summed up later like this:

'*What could be worse? And at the same time what could be more magnificent?*'

54

At the end of it all he wondered over and over again what Poussin would have said if he had been there with us, and seen his work on the wall, and listened to everything.

'*He would probably have been very pleased*' said Picasso.

The Warriors appeared in Picasso's work at a very characteristic period of the history of the painting of our time. It was the history at once eventful and dull, but the far-stretching pastures of abstract art were beginning to be cropped, their delicate flowers were becoming monotonous and their grass becoming sparse. In a word, that great faceless freedom was going out of fashion. The long international miles of exactly similar paintings were beginning to pall. That does not mean that they were being replaced by anything better or that there was any improvement in normal representative art, or that anyone could recognize the old paintings which reappeared with new labels.

In any case, during the winter of 1962–63, the thing which certain painters held in such horror as a 'return to subject painting' (consequently to the worst aspects of the subject, according to them) was carried on quite naturally by Picasso as a continuation of himself.

We can talk about it now that we can see it all from some distance. Up to that point we could not *write* on the subject what Picasso *said* on the subject.

It is one thing to give one's views in the intimacy of the studio, and another to use these conversations—which have gone on for so many years—as arguments in the murder of innocent painters on both sides or to fan the fury of useless discussions.

For Picasso, then, the *avant-garde* is always *en avant*. It's a rare thing and must be sought elsewhere. Far away. Where no one has ever been.

For him, it is a long time since the last drop was squeezed from abstract art; a very long time. And everything which has been called abstract art since then appears anachronistic. He himself had stuck objects on to a canvas, and used anything he could pick up, a long time ago, and the new realism

55

might well appear obsolete and above all ephemeral; it's a thing you do once and then stop.

And so on.

But abstract art and the way it spread unchecked over the continents, the writings on the subject, the ravings, the abuse made of the words 'inner self' (as though Van Gogh had been a photographer without an inner self) and 'absolute freedom' (as though painting had only one: the freedom not to 'represent', which reduces a painter's freedom to very little)—all this weighed heavily on painting and for years haunted many of our conversations with Picasso.

Picasso, who dared to paint the cruel warrior, the innocent child, the ravaged woman, and to say what he had to say on the subject.

The first time we went into the studio with the 'Warriors', where there were heads of 'Warriors' on the floor, in the background the great blue man playing the pipe, the top, just glimpsed, of a mountain landscape, the corner of the 'Still life with cat', and a heap of other canvases piled everywhere, and on the easel the tall canvas in black and white—or almost—with, at the bottom, the woman with inverted breasts—a great burst of painting, challenging and free—the first time he showed us this enormous sum of work and research more difficult than he had ever known before, and yet spread over so little time and with such perfect success, we stayed for a long time, gazing, entering into it. (It was one of those happy moments his friends know so well, when Picasso comes and goes, pulling and pushing canvases, leaning them one against the other and moving back to see them, with that way he has of examining whoever is looking on, and realizing at once whether or not he can see in his face what he has tried to bring to life there.)

As we left, Picasso stopped on the threshold, giving one last glance to the canvases before going out, an anxious, questioning glance.

He closed the door on them with a sigh of relief, and said:

'I'm trying to understand. I'm trying to get inside So-and-so's skin, for example' (mentioning the name of an abstract painter) 'But what a life! What can he think about in his studio, all alone in front of his easel? . . . When you think he's been painting the same picture for ten years! . . . It's a question that really worries me. What on earth can he find to think about? . . . He must be bored to death! . . .'

He added a little later on:

'At least if I come a cropper I know afterwards how it happened, and often I end by knowing why. Perhaps I've learnt something. And perhaps this might even be the time when I think I've crashed and I haven't crashed at all. In any case nobody can say I haven't tried. He paints, and that's his business, and if he likes that, then perhaps he's the one that's right. But as a way of painting, it's a bit like going off on the 8.15 every morning.'

For Picasso the moralist is a moralist also in painting. Everything hangs together. It isn't a case of what one is and what one paints, there's just one painter, first and last. It isn't the man who commits himself and the painter who paints; it is a single way of life and work adopted by one head which is also the same heart, the same eye and the same hand.

For Picasso painting is never a game. It is for him the most serious thing in the world. It is the very breath of life to him.

If his painting stopped beating, he would die.

This sort of exhalation of the man towards the canvas and of the will of the canvas upon the man, which people call painting, he calls a matter of life and death.

And it is as true as it is for the matador.

Thus he demands from painting the most violent efforts, and insists that painting itself should not be put up for sale in every market place by people using it for purposes that have nothing to do with art, and filling it with all sorts of ingredients on which it is bound to choke.

It is not a question of good painters and bad painters; he loves all painters—or almost—and respects them even when they are wrong. For in this trade, he says, there is '*a kind of*

madness which deserves to be taken into consideration. Even
if it's a landscape with ducks we are concerned with, or, on
the other hand, one brush-stroke on top of another brush-
stroke.'

But in some things this century, more than any other, has
exceeded all bounds. Painting is treated with contempt, turned
into a peep-show and enslaved to fairground barkers. Convention is exalted as liberty, and soothing-syrup as heady
wine, and anything repeated to infinity, and certainly not
discovered yesterday, is called *avant-garde*. (If people want to
enthrone formulists of representation or non-representation,
we can let that pass—it has always been done). And above
all, for outsiders, painting has for years and years had this air
of facility and abandon. Painting cannot live in such a climate
without suffering. It suffers in all true painters.

And so a painter must be more solitary, more single-minded
than ever. And laugh at what the world may say when he
paints representatively at a time when nobody is doing it,
for example (I mean another kind of representation from the
one he himself has always done; but representation all the
same).

He must do his work.

He must be always seeking.

He must never be content with himself.

He must not consider painting as an art, but as a way of
life.

He must listen to nobody and let himself be influenced by
nothing.

He must be a painter before everything else, and live a
painter's life. All the rest are mere appurtenances. He must
never be on the fringes of his time, for painting is also en-
dowed with power.

If we could draw a moral from the way of life of a man
who never says anything like that, but proves it, that is
probably how we should express it.

That winter several journeys led us towards Picasso's Warriors. On each visit we witnessed the same performance. An

atmosphere of heavy preoccupation, the studio door shut. For example, the night of our arrival. We are aware that unknown canvases are waiting behind that door. That closed door weighs upon us, as always when Picasso is in the throes of battle with his canvases.

And it is such a magnificent trait in his character, this eternal doubt, this question-mark which he drives deep into his innermost being (in this century when, by reason of senseless panegyrics and the metaphysical or financial necessity to 'surpass', there are so many geniuses that nobody knows any more where the painters are).

Picasso is taking a new mountain by storm, and battling against terrible doubts.

He dare not open the studio door.

As soon as he comes out, he moves right away from it.

He knows that the moment he goes in everything will start going badly again.

At that moment he will glance at the warriors in progress. His look will last a hundredth of a second, and it will be decisive. Everything will collapse around him or, on the other hand, the fires will be calmed.

And he hesitates, his hand on the door.

At that moment, it seems quite natural to us. This man, of such consummate arrogance, has so accustomed us to the absolute truth of the doubts he feels about himself that we suffer with him, begging the hidden canvases to be such that he can show himself satisfied with them.

He has worked on them all day, and, he says, he left the studio an utter wreck, knowing nothing, seeing nothing, and ready to smash everything up rather than begin again.

He says to Pignon: '*I hope you're proud of yourself—you've got me into a pretty mess.*'

Upon which he enters the studio as though it were Hell itself, and shuts the door.

And doesn't come out.

He has put everything into these canvases. The eternal 'Guernica' of his soul and its eternal scream. The eternal 'War

59

and Peace' of his soul, and the warriors of death, inexorable as the iron of their helmets and as their stone faces, ferocity pounding through the hooves of their horses.

It is a wild confusion. All Picasso is piled upon Picasso, everything, higher and higher. The horror of war, the virility of the warrior in his strength and of the horse, and even an idea of the warrior-judge whose helmet begins to look like a Phrygian cap, a warrior who resembles the Peace of Vallauris, an air of the rape of the Sabines and an air of the Sabines intervening, temples like arenas, shields like suns, helmets like Romans, horsemen in the distance, swarms of child-corpses, justice, injustice, and above all, above all this distribution of death in which man habitually becomes involved without at last learning not to make use of something which will inevitably fall upon him too.

Picasso's morality admits all of man, except death.

And at the same time his diatribe is against death. The Massacre of the Innocents and the Accident come into being at the same time.

Death is a warrior whose foot crushes. And the symbol is a symbol no more, it has the everyday face of the girl spread-eagled under the sandalled foot of death that rests on her, or the warrior of death above her with his white horse.

There are even combined massacres in which everything is mingled, temples, warriors, horses, women, innocents, and in the foreground the bicycle spreadeagled on the spread-eagled woman. With fresh, sun-bright colours. The girl has a spotted dress.

Pensively, Picasso gazes at the accumulation of his work. He searches for the secrets he has just put into it. He questions himself, painfully. He tortures himself and reassures himself and could kill himself for not being able to qualify for himself, on the spot and infallibly, what he is doing.

He tortures himself and us, tries to open our hearts, to extract from us willy-nilly the truth of the effect which the canvases produce on us, or on ayone else. He tries to make us repeat the exact note of our impression. He tries to find in our eyes, on our lips, in our attitude, in our silence or in our words, the reality of our thoughts. He kills us. He massacres us. And at the same time he jokes. It is a terrifying game.

We are the public.

So we are important.

As important as anyone.

At last the torture ceases in a silence in which everyone gazes.

They are magnificent moments.

Exhausting.

'*What an experience!*' he says.

The most terrible work was done on the canvas in colours, greater in height than in breadth, in which the two warriors face each other.

'*That one*', he said, '*nearly finished me.*'

I remember that one day as we left the studio, he was abruptly cheered by one of those mysterious thoughts which dwell in him and make him appear suddenly relaxed, while we were exhausted with having gazed intently for a long time at so many works and asked them so many questions, and he said: '*After all, you can say what you like, but in any case nobody can say I haven't worked.*'

He said that in the tone of voice of a child who is uncertain of the solution to his problem but has covered pages and pages with calculations.

And he suddenly added '*After all, when people talk about abstract art, they always say that it's music. When they want to praise it they talk about music. Everything becomes music . .*'

As he closed the door on his Warriors whose disappearance lightened his heart for a moment, he finished triumphantly:

'*I think that's why I don't like music.*'

## PICASSO THE MORALIST (continued)

Lying in peaceful rows on the ground, imprisoned in the gilded hexagons of ceramic tiles, devils or fauns—in a word, men—with all their virility displayed, ardently pursue, utterly bent on rape, dishevelled, fleeing, terrified nymphs, with all their charms unfurled—in a word, women.

These mad sarabands of breasts, hair, sexual organs, beards, rumps, with little spots that are nails at the extremities, are all contained in a small tile. '*It would be nice to have whole rooms tiled like that*' said Picasso.

He made these tiles during an August week in 1962. Not one woman or nymph is willing. But it is obvious that the man, the devil, the faun is going to have the last word. No fleeing beauty will long escape such weapons, nor so deliberately aggressive a will. Nor one so triumphant.

Yesterday, a grey autumn day, I went for a long walk with a friend in the park of Versailles, going down towards the great canal and the Trianon, among the golden trees, in a divine solitude soon to become a little sad.

Fortunately there were statues, their presence made more charming than usual by the deserted park; quantities of Herculeses and Apollos, all sorts of friendly gods, more pleasant to encounter than the silence of the paths. Their perfectly placed vine-leaves, much more closely fitting than the scallop-shells of athletes, gave their silhouettes a hermaphroditic softness.

Hercules himself, despite his club and his Nemean lion—never forgotten—took on a sort of plushy angel-air perfectly in tune with his nature as a Versailles statue, poor Hercules!

Picasso would have laughed at me if he had known that, walking austerely in this cold and lonely park (but with my eyes fixed on the statues' vine-leaves like a cartoon lady in an art-gallery) I was thinking of the part played by sex in

Picasso's painting; and here I am not speaking of man and woman but of their attributes.

It is an enormous part. And quite obvious; realistic in short. I mean that the part they play is not greater than that of which nature has made them worthy. . . .

In Picasso's painting, everything conforms naturally to reality, including that which occupies first place in either man or woman.

The sex of a woman, her eye, her hand, her foot, can claim equal consideration on the part of their creator.

In the same way as the eyes in the faces on Picasso's canvases move, are lengthened, stand up vertically or turn their backs on each other, are like flowers or fish, loom over each other like waves or are superimposed like crosses; as noses are unfurled, display their profile or their nostrils, open out, divide, sit or lie on the face, all this with a fervid reality, a truer truth, a freer poetry—in the same way the sexual organs play their painted part as in the work of no other artist. With the same naturalness. With the same ease. As only perhaps the poets can.

And day-dreaming about Picasso and all this, and about the poets, makes me think of Apollinaire, of whom Picasso speaks so often, as he does of Max Jacob. '*And Salmon?*' he always says to me when I arrive.

Hearing him speak of that time of the poets, you can see the youth of all of them begetting that infinite freedom which made them what they are. If Picasso sings a song '*of Max's*' or talks about Apollinaire, something happens which takes you beyond time. You're somewhere else. It's something un-curbed, generous, overflowing, streaming with creativity, a mad whirl of words and ideas where truth takes its place quite naturally before bursting upon us.

'Shadows of my love.' I am thinking of those poems of Apollinaire where Lou's breasts and 'rosy buttocks' blossom in the soldier poet's songs, amid the horrors of war.

> · '*O gracieuse et callipyge*
> *Tous les culs sont de la Saint Jean. . . .*'

This rosy ardour of love which suffers when it blooms and can only imagine, in the midst of death, the wonder of loving a woman—all women—and weaving a dream of rosy skin among the cannons and the trenches, all this unfolds in the poems, love and desire increasing tenfold the bitterness of death, and death multiplying the imagination of love. . . . While nearer and nearer comes the moment which Apollinaire prophetically calls in those same poems 'the fatal spurting of my blood upon the world'.

There was so much of Picasso in Apollinaire, and there is so much of Apollinaire in Picasso.

The satyr of love and the man at war are the same person, there in both of them, the man at war and the man in everything.

Whether they are making love or war, Picasso's men and women show quite naturally that they are not angels. For Matisse, the sex slipped away, disappeared between the thighs of the odalisque. It existed mainly in harmonies, colours and arabesques, and most of the time was only a point of intersection of the body, rarely did it tell its name.

Matisse's admirable nudes have no sex, as they have no expression. Picasso's nudes have an expression and a sex. The sex of the nude is for him an indispensable part of this body, the reality of which he is seeking; this looks like an obvious truth; and yet sexual modesty has for centuries been putting all bodies on the same level. In spite of that nobody has ever thought of levelling in the face that salient and purposeful appendage, the nose.

For Picasso, the sex organ, in painting and in reality, is a sign as constantly recurring as the eye, it is the eye of the body, its crucial point; it is a flower of paint which blossoms in streaks, spots or colours at the end of the stem which takes root where the legs meet. It belongs always to a lover and a poet, unfettered and free from misapprehensions.

And when Picasso sings of love, he doesn't beat about the bush; he flies straight to its centre. Besides, he has, on top of everything else, that Spanish verve, that happiness in the blossoming of love, and the unending wonder of that utter freedom, that capacity for unbridled life which gives his work such pulsating strength.

One day, Picasso wanted to please a friend. He said to him:

'*I'm going to do a drawing for you.*'

'Marvellous!'

'*What sort of a drawing would you like me to do for you?*'

'I'd like a drawing about love.'

Picasso drew a man and a woman making love. There is in Picasso, as in every being that loves love, a sort of tender emotion in the presence of love, which filled this drawing with warmth and tenderness.

'But what am I going to do?' said the friend, embarrassed. 'I shan't dare to show it to anyone, or hang it up.'

He kept it hidden for years before he dared. When the drawing was shown openly it never shocked anyone.

Picasso recalled this incident for a long time; he thought it horrible.

And when someone said one day, apropos of I can't remember what, that there cannot be any modesty in art, he replied that it was possible to paint anything at all, provided that it really was painting.

*It's only when it has nothing to do with painting,* he said, *that there can be any violation of modesty.*

The whole of Picasso's painting is a kind of painting which glorifies virility, and not only glorifies it, but associates it, as is natural, with power, violence, and ultimately destruction and victory.

He would not leave a man's sexual organ out of a painting, any more than he would a woman's breast.

All the bulls in his work proudly parade the attributes which make their power.

All the terrible horses of warriors and wars wage their own stallion-war against men; they trample on humanity with phallus flying, warrior and horse together.

65

There lies their strength and the symbol of their conquest.

The bull in the arena, without the signs of his power, becomes the ox ripe for slaughter which some make of him. But as he is a bull, there lies the secret of his endless blind fury and his indomitable courage.

There remains love, and, God knows, Picasso's work is impregnated with it, because love is life itself. With all the resources and all the materials of his trade, he has given birth to an infinite crowd of lovers, centaurs, nymphs, gods, beauties, men and women, Spanish ladies and matadors, nudes lunching *sur l'herbe*, women of Algiers, great nudes standing, sitting, reclining, drawings by the thousand where couples everlastingly seek for love and become drunk on it.

And yet there is nothing more chaste than painting, nor than the painter as he paints. We need only look at 'The painter and his model'. The model is always naked. Like reality. The painter is always austere in his painter's clothes, behind his painter's easel, concerned only with his problem— that of a painter contemplating a nude. Even if the atmosphere of love in which the painter may live fills his cup to overflowing and gives him that wealth of love-endowed days with which nothing can compare, the canvas hems him in and holds him apart. And then, within this canvas, at the heart of the strange world of the painter at work, we find expressed, entirely in paint, the truth about love.

The world reproaches Picasso—and has still a very long time to spend not reproaching him—with his free representation of the human figure, and with that emancipation which he gives to the features of the face and body in order better to express their life.

Yet no one in the world has exalted woman and her womanliness, her beauty and fragility, her sweetness and her maternity, as he has. He stands for ever in wonderment before that body and sings unendingly of it. And unendingly he questions it. And it is always that body for which he weeps, and which he twists and rends in the disasters of war or the massacre of the innocents. And it is always that body which he would rather paint than anything else in the world.

When Picasso painted the series of 'Déjeuners sur l'herbe', the exhibition opened in Paris with the canvases on one side and the drawings on the other.

During that time the 'Déjeuners sur l'herbe' in the studio at Mougins continued to grow and multiply.

When we talked to Picasso on the telephone from Paris to Mougins and told him about his exhibitions and their private views, he always replied: '*But you know it's still going on here. It hasn't stopped!*' He was drawing and drawing 'Déjeuners sur l'herbe'. He drew and painted so many that all the characters taking part in them began to live their own lives, and to exist, with the particular characteristics which the drawings gave them, from one 'Déjeuner sur l'herbe' to the next.

Between those beautiful rustic nudes and those bearded intellectuals, always busy talking, with their eloquent hands, their walking-canes and their hats, the inevitable happened one fine day. '*It's even astonishing*', said Picasso, '*that it didn't happen sooner.*' Picasso's Manet-nude was at last to fall prey to these fine talkers, fully dressed as they were. At the very least they were to pay court to her . . . visibly.

'*You can't imagine what's happening*', said Picasso. '*Horrible things! . . .*'

And thus ended, quite naturally, the long austere conversation on the picnic grass, between the nudes and the gentlemen.

## THE JACQUELINES

Jacqueline has to an unimaginable degree the gift of becoming painting. She has within her that power on which a painter is nourished. She is the fountain-head. She is made for it, and she submits, and dedicates herself to it and dies in harness, living all the time and never posing. She secretes within her this multiplicity of herself. She peoples Notre-Dame de Vie with her hundred thousand possibilities. She unfolds to infinity. She invades everything, becomes everybody. She takes the place of all the models of all the painters on all the canvases. All the portraits are like her, even if they are not like each other. All the heads are hers and there are a thousand different ones. All the eyes are black, all the breasts are rounded; it is raining Jacquelines all through the house, and whichever way you turn she is looking at you. Sometimes it is almost a portrait, sometimes not at all. She is that enormous nude or that delicate one, that epitome of woman or that long exposition of femininity. She is sitting, lying, standing, everywhere. She is dreaming, thinking, playing. During these twelve years of Picasso's life, painting and love have mated and mingled. All this unbridled output of Jacqueline, from the portrait of Madame Z . . . and the reading woman of the 'Mystère Picasso' down to the last models of the last painters with their paint still wet, has been growing from day to day. The enormous vitality of the painter feeds on this face which is itself painting, and vice versa. It is the Song of Songs of Notre-Dame de Vie.

## THE STUDIO WITHOUT WALLS

In his house of Notre-Dame de Vie, Picasso wants his studios to grow and multiply. It is true that he has never done so much work. First of all he set up a studio (two walls and a roof) on a terrace.

Then he set up another studio on the roof of the first, below the level of his bedroom, a window of which opens into it like a theatre. From the sea to the Estérel, all the hills, all the roads, all the boats are at home there through the glass walls. He says he would like a studio without walls at all, without glass, without anything. He could paint in it as though he were out of doors.

## THE SOUND BARRIER

*People have started to talk about painting, says Picasso, as though it were a competition to see who can go the farthest. But what does it mean, farthest? . . . When it's painting you're talking about, what does it mean, breaking the sound barrier with a canvas? Does it mean doing nothing more on it? Or doing anything, no matter what? Or else does it mean being Van Gogh?*

## THE BLACKNESS OF NOTHING

Picasso relates that a painter friend of his father said to him over and over again: '*And if you see nothing, you use black.*'

*Picasso says . . .*

## THE INNER SELF

Picasso says: '*My inner self is bound to be in my canvas, since I'm the one doing it. I don't need to worry about that. Whatever I do, it'll be there. In fact, there'll be too much of it. It's all the rest that's the problem!*'

## LESS AND LESS

All the features of a face and a body can exist in the eyes of the onlooker, whereas on the canvas not one of them is the shape of a nose, a mouth or a breast.

The stroke or the spot, its shape, its colour and their relationships have a 'charge' of reality. Picasso, in this winter of 1964, seems to be seeking to bring a face into being without description, enumeration, transposition, deformation or anything that makes a face, but bearing the charge of that face.

That is why he says: '*At this moment, on these canvases, I'm doing less and less.*'

## TRUTH?

'What truth?' says Picasso. '*Truth cannot exist. If I look for truth in my canvas, I can do a hundred canvases with this truth. Which, then, is the true one? And who is truth? The one who serves as my model or the one I paint? No, it's like everything else. Truth does not exist.*'

'I remember', says Paulo Picasso, 'that when I was very small, I always used to hear you say: "Truth is a lie . . ."'

## TECHNIQUE

Conversation turns on the power to search freely which a superlative technique gives to the artist.

'Yes', says Picasso. 'But provided that you have so much that it completely ceases to exist. It disappears. At that point, yes, it is important to have it. Because it does everything it has to do, and you only have to bother about what you are seeking.'

## LITTLE LOUIS

Picasso tells how people of all trades used to come to the Bateau Lavoir in the Rue Ravignan, people from the neighbourhood, actors, ladies and gentlemen, and beggars.

One of the latter was called Little Louis.

'He was the same age as us', says Picasso.

He loved to come to the studio.

'He stayed there sometimes all day. He watched me working. He loved that.'

. . . And I wondered whether Little Louis (who died his vagrant's death in his prime) had one day been present at the birth of the 'Demoiselles d'Avignon'.

## THE SAME THING

Picasso tries to make each brush-stroke one unit of painting. He doesn't want design on one side and colour on the other. Or the design of the colour and the colour of the design.

In the end, when we come to look at them, *design and colour must be the same thing.*

## CÉZANNE AND TINTORETTO

*A great thing in modern painting, says Picasso, is this. A painter like Tintoretto, for example, begins his canvas, and then he goes on, and finally when he has filled it and worked all over it, only then is the canvas finished.*

*Whereas if you take a canvas by Cézanne (and you can see it even better in the water-colours) as soon as he begins to make the first stroke the picture is already there.*

## THE CHAINS OF FREEDOM

*Freedom, says Picasso, is something you have to be very careful about. Whatever you do you find yourself in chains. The freedom not to do something means that you're absolutely bound to do something else. And there are your chains. It reminds me of Jarry's story about the libertarian soldiers on parade. The command was given: Right turn! And immediately, because they were libertarians, they were all obliged to turn left. Painting is like that. You take freedom and shut*

72

*it up with your idea, just that one and no other. And there you are in chains again.*

## FREEDOM AND CHILDREN'S DRAWINGS

Still on the subject of freedom and the chains it implies.

Picasso rises in revolt. He says: *They tell you that you have to give children freedom. In reality they make them do children's drawings. They teach them to do it. They have even taught them to do children's drawings which are abstract . . .*

*In reality, as usual, on the pretext of giving them complete freedom and above all not tying them down, they shut them up in their own special style, with all their chains.*

*An odd thing*, he adds, *is that I have never done children's drawings. Never. Even when I was very small. I remember one of my first drawings. I was perhaps six, or even less. In my father's house there was a statue of Hercules with his club in the corridor, and I drew Hercules. But it wasn't a child's drawing. It was a real drawing, representing Hercules with his club.*

## 'AFTER SO-AND-SO'

'What does it mean', says Picasso, 'for a painter, to paint "after So-and-so" or to imitate someone else? What's wrong with it? On the contrary, it's a good thing. You must always be trying to imitate somebody else. But the fact is, you can't! . . . You would like to! You try! But you make a botch of the whole thing . . . And it's at that point that you make a botch of everything you are yourself.'

73

## FOR AND AGAINST

Picasso says that when you're working you must always be against. Everything you do must be against. And never for. *'From the moment you start being for, it's all up with you'*, he says.

## THE SEED

A discussion starts on the difficulty of saying, writing, respecting or reproducing someone's words. And on the different methods which different people use to achieve this.

'It's all the more difficult', says Picasso, 'because if you take a sentence which has been uttered, and write it down exactly, in the same words, it becomes something else altogether, and often the opposite of what it was.'

'Jacqueline says', he adds, 'that when you speak it's like sowing seeds. Sometimes the seeds germinate and flourish. Sometimes they disappear.'

## PAINTING IS NOT INOFFENSIVE

On the subject of the irritating habit which some people have of considering that painting isn't of any consequence in the long run, that 'this animal is not dangerous', Picasso exclaims:

'You must be very careful about that. It's all very fine to paint a portrait with all the coat buttons and even the button-

holes, and the little highlights on the buttons. But watch out!
... There comes a moment when the buttons start flying in
your face ...'

## THE PORTFOLIO OF DRAWINGS

Late at night, a portfolio of drawings was placed on a chair.
For a long time we looked at the hundreds of drawings which
were also the source of new work. They ought to be shown,
these thousands of drawings. They are moreover the secret
leaven of everything.

'And then at once they become something else', says Picasso.
'They have to be taken out, framed, put under glass and hung
on the wall of a room ... You must see them in the portfolio.
Otherwise everything's changed! ...'

But alas! ...

## BRAQUE AND INTENTION

*Braque always said that in painting only the intention counts,*
says Picasso. *And it's true. It's what you want to do that
counts, not what you do. That's what's important. In cubism,
the most important thing of all in the end was what they
wanted to do, the intention they had. And that's something
you can't paint.*

*Picasso says . . .*

## 'NUDE'

'What I'm looking for at the moment', says Picasso, 'is a sign that says "blank" on my canvas, immediately, without any fuss!'

## SUNSET

Picasso called us on to the little terrace where he paints. A vast rosy landscape enveloped us, receding to an infinite distance, suffusing the sky and the sea far in the background. It was a sublime fairyland; nature took precedence over everything, and we looked at her as though we did not know her.

It was only sunset over Cannes, the sea and the Estérel. 'I've never painted that', said Picasso. 'I really shall have to get down to it one day!'

## THE GIFT OF METAMORPHOSIS

Picasso was talking about the famous saddle and the famous bicycle handlebars which he joined together to make a bull's head.

He said: 'One day I take the saddle and the handlebars, I put them one on top of the other, and I make a bull's head. All well and good. But what I should have done straight after was to throw away the bull's head. Throw it into the street, into the gutter, anywhere, but throw it away. Then a workman comes along. He picks it up. He thinks that with this bull's *head he could perhaps make a saddle and a set of bicycle handlebars. And he does it . . . That would have been magnificent. It is the gift of metamorphosis.'*

## PICASSO'S CORRIDA

Summer 1965: the corridas of Frejus. The corrida of the dead horse. The corrida when none of the banderillas managed to stay on the bull; they all fell out. (Arias said he'd never seen that happen). The corrida of the yellow-red bull who knew too much for a bull. The corrida of El Cordobes, with the people mad with ecstasy, yelling, exulting, booing.

(Arias is a friend of Picasso's. Spanish. A hairdresser at Vallauris. He never misses a corrida.)

The picador misses his aim. The people shout. Sneer. Say 'butchery!' and say 'enough!' 'They think', says Arias, 'that it's like pricking an olive in a saucer with a cocktail stick when you're drinking your apéritif.'

The bull is dead. But he is still alive. He can still kill. He gets up, dead. The peones run round and round him, their capes flying in the wind. The matador stands straight, waiting. But the bull does not fall. He lies down, dead, yet living.

The matador lunges and thrusts. The bull's head moves again. The people yell. He thrusts again. It moves. Blood flows from the muzzle. 'The sword is in his lung' says the aficionado. The bull's eyes are still alive. His blood is red with a redness to be seen only here—on his black bull's flank in the sun. The clotted blood makes lacy patterns on its edges. The crowd of men wax facetious and consign the matador to the slaughterhouse, the pork-butcher's, the bacon-slicer. And the crowd of women, crammed with olés, hide their eyes so as not to see. 'Enough! Enough!' they say.

That is the corrida.

And all this time the young men on the highest arches walk upon the sky, everything glows with the bright colours of the shirts; the men selling beer and paper hats sway on the rope of the tiers with their cries on their lips and their baskets for a balancing pole. The French and American police are in the first boxes in the corridor, with photographers whose cameras click behind drapes of light. The matador comes and pulls himself up with his elbows on the barrier. He offers his bull to Picasso. For glory. For friendship. For Spain. There was a matador this summer who was also at Malaga. He said he hoped to do honour to Picasso. Who listened to him, standing. Thanked him. And caught his hat, which he placed in front of him. It is as hot as an oven in the arena under the open sky, and everyone roars with laughter when the toreadors leap the barrier, fleeeing from the bull in his still-fresh fury as he pounds across the arena and beats with his horns on the wood. Paws the ground. Bellows. Charges. Such a proud neck. A big one, that. 'Oh, but his horns are filed, I assure you.' Says the aficionado.

That is the corrida.

The bull charges. The matador turns. Lifts his cape. Shouts. The bull passes. Ah! That was a near one. The cape flies out. The bull passes. The matador turns. A movement like fire. He calls. Feet together. Motionless. Passes the bull like a thunderbolt. Bravo! The aficionado gives the name of the pass. Olé. The bull's thunderbolt strikes the matador. The matador lies prone, his head between his arms, and the black bull, a ribbon of blood streaming from the wound on his flank, imprisons him between the half-ton-weight of his hooves and his horns of a thousand deaths, and all around the whole arena bristles with toreadors running, waving capes, distracting the bull, calling. And the bull comes, thanks be to the gods in heaven. The crowd is on its feet, yelling. Shouts of pity, fear, horror. But the bull rushes in another direction. The matador has got up. He shakes himself. Takes the cape which someone holds out to him. The sword. Walks towards the bull, limping a little. With his hand sweeps aside the peones who widen their circle, moving backwards. The bull charges. The cape. Pass. Olé. Pass. Olé. Pass. Olé. The mad crowd yells with admiration. Yells. Olé. Yells. Olé. Claps. Loudly. Until its hands hurt. A wild enthusiasm.

The bull does not move. The matador stands on tiptoe.

'It's too soon!' Shouts the aficionado. 'He isn't standing square to him.'

The matador stikes. The sword flies into the air.

The crowd tells the matador to go and keep cows. Kill calves. Slice bacon. Assassin! Assassin! Butcher!

That is the corrida.

And afterwards he kills the bull. And he gets an ear. And he walks round the arena with his arched matador's step, heel in the sand, foot lifted, leg raised in a curve. Drinks from the flasks thrown to him. Holds the flowers. Throws back the shoes. Walks in front of his own people in a halo of bravos, the sun of victory.

That is the corrida.

All this time Picasso has said nothing. Only a few words from time to time, always the same words, pointing to the matadors when they enter the arena behind the alguacils, crossing themselves, the banderillero standing within the horns of his lifted arms, the matador's walk, his winged dance-step with the bull.

A few words: 'How pretty it all is . . .'

And afterwards he goes away. The festival is over.

We must not think that the place the corrida holds in his life is merely a part of the Spanish tradition of Spaniards.

It is that too.

Or in the Goyesque tradition which normally demands that a Spanish painter should love bulls.

At the same time it is all that too. As it always is with Picasso, of whom no one can ever say: 'it is thus and not otherwise'.

But there is something more. Elsewhere. Something wordless. Something, first of all, which makes Picasso no more a Spanish painter than Van Gogh is a Dutch painter. That is to say, he is Spanish in the same way as Van Gogh is Dutch. That is to say, he is Spanish. But he is above all Picasso, as Van Gogh is Van Gogh.

And the Spanish corrida of Fréjus, Arles or Nîmes, with bulls from the Camargue or Madrid, with a thousand Spanish features or none at all, is above all *related* to him. It is something in him which is as much a part of his life as going up to the studio. He dresses in his best and goes with his wife and it is the festival of the sun. But all the rest of the time, too, the spirit of the corrida is part of his way of life. He has bulls in his soul. The matadors are his cousins. The arena is his house.

## THE PAINTER AND HIS MODEL

The 'Warriors' are finished, all over—enough of Sabine women and massacres! *'All we have to do now is put one in the pillory at the Salon de Mai'*, says Picasso.

If, however, he doesn't change his mind in the meantime. For now that we are at the end of so well-filled an autumn, he still goes on saying that he does not know what to think of these warriors.

Does one ever know what one is doing? Can any moral be drawn from it?

Can anyone in the world give a painter certainty? Nevertheless, the 'Sabine Women' are making the conquest of surprised visitors. Picasso relaxes a little when he thinks he catches in a voice the sound of truth. He comes out of the studio with his usual: *'Ah well, if you like it, I'm glad'* which is a sign not of a lifting of his own doubts, but of a sort of transient pleasure. It is enough to see him looking at his warriors, to understand, that in spite of everything all his torment about them is far from being soothed. One day he even uttered this fine painter's phrase: '*But as for them, they say nothing!*'

And we suddenly looked at the canvases with different eyes.

There is nothing stranger and more enchanting than the sight of this confrontation of the creator and his creation. In the work there is silence, in the painter, doubt.

As though the work and the painter were neither the same man, nor the same canvas.

After that came a short time during which Picasso did a bit of everything. It was winter at Mougins. He said '*The warriors are in the cupboard*'. He worked. Life is austere at Notre-Dame de Vie, even when a greenhouse gaiety of colour and the warmth of the sun brood over love and work. Apart from the beach in summer and a corrida from time to time, they go out little, work eats up the days, and indeed a moment must have a quality without equal—and that is rare—for the pleasure it gives to surpass that of enclosing themselves in solitude, the painter and his model, at Notre-Dame de Vie. Then, for the two together, everything becomes a delightful adventure.

It was snowing at Mougins. Jacqueline got behind the wheel one Sunday and drove Picasso at random among the little mountains which you meet as soon as you turn your back on the coast, and which are so pretty with their steep slopes, gorges, passes, woodland and scrub.

Then they lived through an adventure. They had frost beneath their wheels and skies of an incredible blue above their heads. They played at being alone in the world and not knowing where they were going. And they were, in fact, lost. They were gay, mad, in love and venturesome. They might have crashed—and they came very near to it—in this magical, snow-clad country which seemed to them the loveliest in the world.

And the loneliest.

(My pen, as they say, is trying to follow the tracks of their story).

81

For they talked for a long time about this excursion as though of a journey to wonderland, an adventure which left in their hearts a love for the unexpected, for freedom and regret. (To help the story on its way, there was even a castle which grew out of the wayside and out of Picasso's memory. They peered at the courtyard through the keyhole, and look! There was a party going on, and they went in all covered with snow, with their heavy shoes, to join the merrymaking of Le Grand Meaulnes).

They returned, happy, to Mougins.

Why tell the story of that excursion? The warriors were sleeping, uncertain like their master. The painters and their models were as yet unborn. But on December 16, 1962, there was this blue canvas in the studio. An exceptional canvas, with is mountains, its icy whiteness, its snowy blueness, and its holes that were lakes.

He proclaimed, proudly: '*I have done a landscape*'.

Five days later, on the last day of the year, the afternoon of December 31, Picasso painted a huge piper sitting with feet apart and elbows raised, on a canvas that was half blue (the sky), and half green (the grass). The man breathed his melody over the universe, and it was a happy canvas and singularly inspired. A prophet was playing the flute. He was as big as the world, and proclaimed a new age.

In January, then, we could see in the studio all the warriors, all their horses and all their heads, all the women and all the children, the cat and the cruel dog and the lobster, and, behind, those blues whose source intrigued us. And which Picasso pulled forward saying that this one was very funny and that he'd done some strange things that winter. He said to Pignon:

*You who are a painter, you know how it happens. You can make the most appalling efforts and sweat blood over your canvases, but nobody's making you do it. On the contrary nobody gives a damn whether you're doing that or something* else. And you always choose the worst thing, even if you know they'd rather have a bunch of flowers. At any rate they don't like it. And even if they like it, you can be sure that it isn't because of the painting. Anyway you, the painter, you've done some work, and that's something; so you're happy. And then you go off and do a landscape or a chap making music. Why? Why that and not Notre-Dame? Or a portrait of my parrot? I'll tell you why. At the moment when you do it, it brings you some sort of release. And that's the essential thing.'

That night in my room I wrote all that down on the pages of a cheap novel, against my usual custom. I did not want to forget these few words about freedom which served as a conclusion. 'You must be very careful what you're doing. Because it's when you think you're least free that you're sometimes the most completely so. And you aren't at all free when you feel you have giant's wings which stop you from walking.'

We now know that after the 'Sabine Women' (and a little random step into the snow of landscape, a man blowing a pipe nobody knows why, just for the unfettered delight of doing what you want to) he was to take possession of the 'Painter and his model' and let himself go as perhaps he never had before.

Were the 'Sabine Women' the hidden cause of it? Had they kept him imprisoned? Or had they, as they set him free for other work, given him the key of all new freedoms? Only he could tell.

As far as he ever says anything very explicitly, he once told us that these child-murderers and kidnappers of Sabine women had been the starting-point from which new painting problems had risen for him.

The 'Warriors' had set him infinite problems. They were bearers of ideas, even anecdotes, murders and shields, they rode the horses of Poussin, David or Picasso, they killed the women of Judaea, Rome, Guernica and all time. Precise ideas gathered them together in public places; the painting spoke of good and evil, cruelty, innocence, pain and weakness.

83

*Picasso says . . .*

It was an extraordinary work-situation. Punishment. And at the same time a miracle. The painter in chains, back to the wall, at bay, the painter once more attacking a formidable theme, bringing the boldest crashing to earth. It was work without indulgence, without let-outs, without facility, without mercy, the work of a man completely welded to his idea, his dangerous idea. He suffered, but at the same time exulted. He was wrapped in gloom, but in the depths of his night gleamed the dawn of conquest.

And now he says he is turning his back on everything. He says he is flinging himself into an incredible adventure. He says everything is changed, it's all over, painting is something quite different from what we believed, perhaps it's even the exact opposite . . .

It was during this period that he declared himself ready to kill modern art, and thus art itself, in order to rediscover painting. It was art, he said, this damned art, that in the long run made the birth of the 'Warriors' so tragic for him. These preconceived ideas people have. These moulds into which they think you can pour everything '*as if you were making cakes*'.

Down with habits!

Down with 'deformation' or 'reformation' or any premeditated notion you like.

Or even not premeditated at all, but instinctive.

That's worse.

'*Because if you can swim and somebody throws you into the water, you swim.*'

'*We have to look*', says Picasso, '*for something that develops all on its own, something natural, and not manufactured, it has to evolve just as it is, in its natural shape and not its shape in art.*'

'*Grass like grass, a tree like a tree and a nude like a nude.*'

Then down with everybody, down with everything that's been done, down with Picasso! For also and at the same time and quite naturally it is Picasso and his painting methods he is attacking.

84

'*We do the same thing over and over again, and yet we can do everything, what is there to stop us?*'

The great quest for freedom has begun again.

Strange freedom! Every time he takes her, submissive, in his arms, she takes advantage of it to imprison him, the creator. Every time he has her he loses her. If he wants to keep her he has to start all over again. For the painter, as for everything else, freedom cannot be the end. It is never more than a stage on the journey.

In February 1963 Picasso broke loose. He painted 'The painter and his model'. And from that moment he painted like a madman. Perhaps he will never paint again with such frenzy.

On February 22nd, he painted a painter seated at the easel. A plaster or stone head, standing on a chest of drawers, watches the painter.

From the 22nd to the 26th he worked on another canvas with the same theme.

On March 2nd, he painted four canvases: the painter and his model with a green nude.

On the 4th he painted a white nude, plus two canvases with the painter's head.

And on the 10th, a canvas of the painter alone in front of his canvas.

On the 13th, the nude is holding a glass at arm's length while the painter goes on working.

On the 14th the nude is elsewhere, sleeping perhaps, at any rate the painter is alone, working at the easel in the studio.

On March 25th, the painter is all alone. On the canvas of the 26th, it is the model's turn to be alone, standing triumphant on a large canvas, and, the same day, on another canvas, the painter is working in front of the bust, which is growing in size, while the model has moved away and looks tiny at the far end of the studio.

On the 27th the nude is becoming larger. On the 28th it

has come near enough to the painter's easel to touch it. On the 29th, the painter puts on his hat. On the 30th his easel and his beard are blue, O Bluebeard of a thousand wives, hung in all the picture-galleries of the world. And the same day the chest of drawers becomes orange for another canvas and the nude takes on vast proportions.

On April 2nd, the Afghan hound Kaboul comes and lies at the painter's feet.

And on the 3rd, the painter puts on a fawn-coloured hat to work.

And the rhythm quickens desperately, the canvases accumulate.

On April 28th, on one canvas, the painter is painting at night by electric light, but on another, the same day, he dresses warmly from top to toe and poses his model naked under the apple-tree in the garden.

On May 1st, there they are, both of them, deep in the forest, but on the same day a green nude on a red chair is posing for the painter in the studio, in the studio where Picasso is painting the painter painting and the model posing.

On the 5th the weather is mild, and the painter is in the garden in summer clothes, painting the nude relaxing in the sun on a chaise-longue.

On the 10th the painter has put Jacqueline's coolie-hat on his head, and posed his model lying in the forest thick with trees.

On the canvas of the 11th they have come back into the studio.

But on the 16th they go out again.

And so on.

All this not counting the portraits of the painter, the heads of a model who is imaginary but Jacqueline, the portrait of the painter's leg with shoe and trouser-leg, the studios with lights in the ceiling or a large glove nailed to the wall.

It's painting at full tilt.

Creation with the brakes off.

Research bursting like a bomb.

It's an orgy of painting after the Ramadan of the Sabine Women.

When he painted 'The painter and his model', Picasso was alone in front of his canvas, in his studio with its phenomenal variety and infinite number of canvases and everything else piled there, looking like nothing on earth but Picasso's studio. The harvests of decade after decade have been garnered there. There are stacks of projectors and easels, the palettes are tables. Picasso never uses a palette.

But the painter's studio on Picasso's canvases is a painter's studio, a 'proper one' as people imagine it when it doesn't really exist. A chest of drawers and sometimes a stand for the bust. A divan for the model to lie on naked. A lamp with its reflector. A chair for painting the model seated, when she doesn't sit on the floor. We see a window with stained glass in it, and sometimes large swelling blank spaces which are studio curtains. One day perhaps a studio screen behind which the model undresses and in front of which she can be silhouetted. Another day a little horse on a shelf, the pretty little jointed wooden horse that stands with bent legs in the windows of painters' colour-merchants, and which painters used to use when drawing walking, trotting or galloping horses.

In this studio, as always in what one calls a studio, the painter is always seated at the easel and we see his canvas in profile. He holds the classic palette and sheaf of brushes, and paints, paints, paints, very upright, with heavy shoes. No one tries to give him any other sort of attitude but that of the painter seated at the easel painting a model who is posing. He is the painter as such, doing his standard job.

The studio, then, is a 'painter's studio', and the painter a 'painter at the easel'. He does not paint standing like Picasso, but he is a serious, careful painter like him. His quest never falters from one canvas to the next. Almost always, as is proper, he has a painter's beard and long painter's hair. Except when, occasionally and by chance, he begins to look like Picasso. Temptation . . .

What the painter is doing, whether he is succeeding, whether it is good or bad, no one knows. We would almost like to look at his canvas and find out. But we only see the model.

And it is Picasso who is painting the model. Or at any rate it is Picasso who displays her. We can't really tell. It's like a dance. The painter is always painting. Picasso is always painting him a model over which he has to cudgel his brains. That isn't surprising; she is changing all the time.

The painter also changes from one canvas to the other. The studio too. Sometimes it disappears completely, and all we see is a lovely coloured floor of a kind that has never existed. Or else everything happens in the sunshine of the garden or the shade of the forest.

The painter changes, but at the same time he is the same. He is a head with an eye, a foot with a shoe, a hand with a brush. He is painted in a thousand ways, he, his chair and his eye. All the lines of his profile and his beard and his body are having the time of their lives, and yet the painter, more or less witty or simple, serious or attentive, beautiful as a god or a painter, with one single little eye in profile or eyes popping out of his head, sitting firmly on his bottom on the chair, firmly upright or firmly leaning, the painter is always the painter, with all the perseverance, all the stability, all the stubbornness he needs.

We are taken in to such an extent that the painter does not appear to present the slightest problem in the canvas . . . He is there. He is doing his job. It's the model that causes all the difficulty and plays him all the tricks; he tries to catch her in vain. While Picasso does catch her. Sometimes by one end, sometimes by the other. Picasso has us so well tamed that we enter into his game, his problem is ours, and we become the painter at his easel, pursuing a model he never succeeds in reaching, and whom Picasso catches repeatedly. Like that, we understand better how inaccessible the model is, and how many thousand times we can catch her and still not have her.

88

'*I want to paint nudes as they are*' says Picasso. Or
'*They have to paint themselves!*'
Or else:
'*I don't want to paint nudes, I want people not to be able to help seeing nudes as they are.*'
Or finally:
'*There comes a moment, if you manage to do what you're trying to, when the breasts fall into place themselves without your even needing to draw them.*'

This beautiful, nonchalant nude, unfolding so naturally on her divan or chaise-longue, a nude so overwhelming to the painter, arrogant, mocking him, with such queenly self-sufficiency, growing in the studio like a tree in the earth, without problems while the painter has so many—this nude which Picasso paints for his poor painter in all her manifold poses and solutions is for him the great two-edged question by which his life as a painter is continually harassed.

The painter's favourite reality is this woman, living, two-fold, whose body can be worked out in a thousand ways by the mind, and felt in a thousand ways by the body.

Always the painter and reality. Always the fanatic with his instruments of torture, his palette, his brushes, the side view of the canvas and his little nails, always the painter, the unfortunate, always there with his eye, watching, asking himself questions. He is in the studio: the temple. Or in nature: the temple multiplied. He works ceaselessly, he kills himself with work. He takes immense pains; he sits and paints, he sits and gazes. Facing him, in the temple of the divan or the chaise-longue or the grass, the woman, the model, peacefully displays herself as she is, knowing her perfection, in the ineffable splendour of her truth, her beauty, the multiplicity of her flesh, her hair, her breasts, an unending kaleidoscope of woman, of buttocks and arms, eyes and toes, endlessly unmade and remade and always, insolently, there. So simple in fact. She is as she is. What difficulty is there? She is that delight in existence and that tranquillity, that open door, that

89

joie de vivre and that voluptuousness, that obviousness against which the painter bruises himself. She is reality without problems. She grows on the canvas with all her woman's attributes, vigorously, as a tree grows in open ground. And just as naturally.

And we see this detachment, this ease, this abandon written all over her. Confronting her with constant anxiety, a prey to his painful obsessions, a poor creature is doing his job.

The eternal painter, eternal votary of the easel, his palette a lyre and his brush a sword, the painter tearing out his eyes and rending his skin, yet apparently motionless at his work, paints his model diligently, one canvas after another. Ah, poor painter!

I'm not thinking one word of all this while I'm looking at the canvas. Only later. But Picasso's way of talking while he shows his canvases suggests it all. He talks a lot about the painter. He speaks of him tenderly, he's a nice painter-chap. A real painter, with a real beard, he says. He says he has even done a few painting their nudes '*in natural surroundings*'. Thousands of painters with their models. '*I've even done his shoe and the crease in his trouser leg*', he says.

It's true. At the bottom of the great canvas facing me there is another little one, showing the lower part of the painter's leg, his trouser leg and his big country shoe. '*Why not?*' says Picasso.

He is a real painter with his heavy shoes on.

And at the same time he is all the painters in the world struggling with their obsessions.

Because when Picasso does painters in studios he paints them all and he paints himself. At the same time he does not show us the work of the painter on the painted painter's canvas; we never see that. But he shows us the painter's model on his, Picasso's, canvas. By painting the unpaintable model he becomes the painter at his easel. When he flings all these woman-elements higgledy-piggledy into the studios, all these triumphant nudes, all these realities nagging at the painter, he is at one and the same time the poor painter struggling with an inaccessible reality, and the painter triumphing over it because he can show it in all its inaccessiblity.

This nude is a patch of green flung on to a divan. A thick black line gives it its essential contours.

There is also a green colour within which a darker line throws up all the necessary masses.

Or else nothing but a peculiarly shaped patch, hair, the little arrow-head of the sex-area, and two dots. A dot is enough to make a breast, a streak for an arm, and so on.

Or perhaps a large blank space across which green spots wander, and then a black one; that's the hair; and the whole body is there.

But all these complicated blue circles have the same effect. This light blue on the red divan becomes a nude, but why? A dot, two lines, a face? Two lines make the knees, and that one has legs.

And these white nudes, standing or lying, are white patches ringed with green, empty spaces in the shape of the essential shapes of the body.

But sometimes all the toes are there, all the nails and eyebrows. And even painted nails, and huge eyes with lashes, and ears, or again a few lines are drawn on a blank space or a red patch, and there, we cannot tell by what miracle, lies the nude, whole and perfect.

He complicates, he simplifies, he searches. Picasso searches. Picasso says:

'I want to SAY a nude. I don't want to make a nude like a nude. I only want to SAY breast, SAY foot, SAY hand, belly. If I can find the way to SAY it, that's enough. I don't want to paint the nude from head to foot, but just to be able to SAY it. That's what I want. When we're talking about it, a single word is enough. Here, one single look and the nude tells you what it is, without a word.'

Picasso said to Pignon:

'We have to find a way of doing a nude AS IT IS.

*Picasso says . . .*

'You have to give whoever is looking at it the means of painting the nude himself with his eyes.

'You know, it's exactly like the barrow-boys. You want a couple of breasts? Right you are, here's a couple . . .

'What you want is for the chap looking at it to have everything handy that he needs to make a nude. If you really give him all the things he needs, and the best, he'll put them in place himself with his eyes. Everyone will make just the nude he wants with the nude I make for him.'

This conversation took place in front of the canvases on May 8, 1963.

'I had to do those ones all myself', said Picasso standing in front of the 'Sabine Women'. 'Nobody helped me . . .'

This was his way of explaining what his problem was that year: one of the manifold stages of his fantastic search for *truth*. The truth of the 'Warriors', which had a subject. The truth of the nudes. The truth of the truth. And even the direction painting must take. Against fashion, against oneself, against every method, against every convention, however modern, against every prohibition of the present time, against and yet with his own knowledge and his capacity for painting no matter what, in no matter what manner and no matter how.

Against reality itself.

For this reality in which everything is set is not, finally, the one which the painter is breaking his heart to express; it is truth which brings that into being. That is the only thing we are searching for today. Modern art has grown infinitely old. It is the modern art of days already long past, remember, when it was for or when it was against reality. Yesterday. Once more, the only thing we seek today is the truth of the world.

Talking, dreaming, listening, we have gradually lost our bearings. In the midst of so many painters and so many studios and so many models. We need to breathe a little. We relax.

And Picasso begins tenderly to show us his last-born among the pictures of 'The painter and his model'. His tenderness is for the painter. He laughs at his little palette. And the care he takes of his painter's beard. And that inimitable seriousness. Even though she is there, luscious, delicious, appetising, within his reach, the wretched creature can do nothing better than to make a little stroke on his little canvas with his little brush.

Poor fellow!

And the painter becomes one of us. Is there anyone who doesn't pity his misfortunes? Anyone who doesn't share his pain? And we laugh at him. Over and above everything else. As always. But it doesn't matter, he goes on. '*He thinks he's going to make out, poor chap!*' says Picasso. And the living painters gaze at the painters on the canvas, sighing with compassion.

The model never poses.

She is Jacqueline as in life.

She never posed for the 'Dames de Mougins' nor the 'Painter and his model', nor the 'Dames de Vauvenargues' nor the 'Dames de la Californie'. But every eye has her eye within it, and every woman has her being.

That is Picasso's way of existence: to be alone in the studio to paint the essential elements of his life.

But this way he has with Jacqueline has become more pronounced. For so many years Jacqueline has always been there, living the same life, creating the same climate, diffusing through this house a special atmosphere, half painting and half love, all painting, all love. The tragedy of painting is hers, and all the canvases have her face. He has put her everywhere, in every colour.

She hangs on every wall. And dozens of her heads cut off at the neck look at you from all sides with their eyes of paint above a cheek of iron.

Picasso's model, who never poses, lives in the midst of the ten thousand canvases he has made of her. She is his imaginary truth, well-known, vividly alive, deeply probed, willing, deserving, beloved and loving.

And I venture to say all this because it very often happens that the canvas is reversed. And—miracle!—Picasso in his studio paints a painter painting his model. The naked model poses for the painter on a couch ready spread for her, as tranquil as though the infinite variety of her body could raise problems for no one. Sure of herself. Of her beauty. As obvious as truth itself.

Sitting behind Picasso, warmly clothed in an armchair, Jacqueline watches Picasso at his easel painting a painter at his easel painting a posing model who is Jacqueline in one of the ten thousand ways the painter has of 'saying' her.

That is how the pictures were painted.

And then came the date of the exhibition. All of that stupendous year went in. There was even added to all those painters, warriors and portraits, a sculpture which Picasso had just had cast in bronze: a woman walking, pushing a pram.

He is passionately fond of this figure, and it is certainly charged with an extraordinary truth, This, all you women, is the mother, proud as Lucifer, unbending and full of the sense of her rights, widespread though they are, and of the prerogatives given her by the successful issue of her maternity: this child in the push-chair, for that is really what it is. She walks, pushing the pram with a movement so true that any mother can recognize herself in it: a position of the fingers you can't mistake, giving the little forward push, holding back at the same time, which is enough to make it move.

The elements of this mother, reduced to a common denominator by the bronze, are those of all the wood-carvings except those which take the form of a woman and a child; she walks in an atmosphere of unusual truth. We know simply by looking at her that she will not even turn her head as she crosses, for she knows that she is the mother, and that everything must move aside before her maternity.

This statue with the child with its rounded limbs stupefies us by its truth. Yet another truth. Another way of expressing it. Where is the only one, the true, the heroic, which has no need of the others? Who is right? Which kills the other?

When the exhibition 'The painter and his model' opened, a bronze mother in a corner was pushing her pram on a stand. The painters were painting, the models were posing, the Warriors on horseback were yelling as they slew the innocents and trampled on the women.

All at once.

And now that we are far away from the painter and his sorrows and his new search which has already begun, we perceive that once the canvases are done there are no more problems. The warriors and the painters whom we had thought scarcely made for war, lived together in admirable harmony. The mother and child fitted them all like a glove. And this truth in the painting, for which they had fought tooth and nail when they were together in the studio, until they almost killed the painter—this truth they bore together, each in his own way.

## THE VISITORS' BOOK

The restaurant proprietor brought the visitors' book. Picasso looked at his painter friend, who was about to oblige, and said: '*Careful! This is the moment of truth!*'

## PETRUSHKA

Picasso loves music that can be seen: hands strumming guitars, Russian, Spanish, Italian folk-tunes when someone sings them before his eyes. He loves flesh and blood music. Richter, when he comes to see him and talk to him. Satie, when he evokes him.

There is however one tune which he often sings, always the same one, and very joyously—an air from 'Petrushka'. And his eyes all light up with the glow of the footlights.

## THE HARLEQUIN-MUSICIANS

In the square. A guitarist and a flute-player come and sit beside Picasso. They play. The guitarist is white and the flautist black. Picasso likes them very much. And besides they are a fine sight on the sand, playing. Picasso says:

*'Whenever I painted harlequin-musicians, that's how I wanted to do them.'*

## FIDELITY

*'Cézanne and Van Gogh', says Picasso, 'didn't for one second mean to do what people see today in Cézanne or in Van Gogh. They only wanted to be faithful to what they saw. They took tremendous pains, and whenever they did something more beautiful than anything else in the world it was only because they couldn't possibly do it any other way—and that's when they became Cézanne and Van Gogh.'*

# FIGURES

You could almost say that the figures in pictures are more easily approachable. In any case they are treated with greater familiarity. Picasso himself comments on their doings with great benevolence and often with tenderness. He points out the little horse in a corner of the painter's studio *'Because from time to time he does a bit of sculpture as well'*, he says. Suddenly, in contrast to the rest of the canvases in which the painter at the easel paints an invisible canvas, the canvas in the picture appears, huge, between the painter and his model, swarming with figures. It takes up practically the whole picture. Picasso speaks of it as the canvas of his fellow-painter, the one in the picture. *'It isn't so bad!'* he says.

# THE REPRODUCTION OF THE PICTURE
# AND
# THE PICTURE OF THE REPRODUCTION

The publisher Spitzer reproduced one of Picasso's canvases and sent him a parcel of prints. Picasso placed in his studio the whole parcel of painters, all exactly alike, pegging away at their easels, brush in hand.

And one after the other he took the reproductions and put them on his easel, brush in hand.

And one after the other he painted them.

Starting from the painter, always the same, at the easel in the reproduction, he painted dozens more. They were full-face or in profile, with or without hats, with or without beards. All very serious, with their little fingers raised, they painted.

*'I could do thousands of them'*, said Picasso. *'It's marvellous to work like this, from a painter who's already there. Basically the most terrible thing of all for a painter is a blank canvas.'*

## THE PALETTE COMPLETED

A clean palette is fixed in position on a wheeled table. It is made of paper and cardboard, fastened underneath with strings.

The other, the old one, is on the ground. An enormously thick layer of paint, one colour on top of another, mixed with crumpled paper which has hardened to form a kind of pattern in relief, gives this palette a most amazing appearance.

'*I'm going to have it framed*', says Picasso. He says that because it is pretty, and not derisively.

## THE PALETTE AND THE RAG

Because it's quite true—the framed palatte could well figure in a Salon. All painters have said or done that, with their palette and the blotting paper they have used on their wash-drawings or water-colours.

'*But never mind*', says Picasso, '*in any case it isn't just any palette, because it's my palette, and so it's something special to me. And if I exhibit this rag, it'll be my own rag on which I've wiped the paint off my brushes. Not my neighbour's rag. And so, for all that, there's something in it that belongs to me.*'

## THE EAGLE OF PROMETHEUS

Picasso says: '*The terrible thing is that everyone is his own Prometheus-eagle, devoured and devouring at the same time.*'
98

## THE SHADOW OF THE PLANT

There is something disturbing, which sometimes even becomes worrying, about the stubborn way in which reality interferes with everything.

'For *example*', says Picasso, showing us a series of canvases leaning against each other edge to edge, '*it's pure chance, but the way that the lines follow on from one canvas to another that was put next to it because it happened to be nearest to hand, is an amazing reality all the same: they're continuing each other!*'

And this?

He shows us a huge green plant in a pot on the ground. On the wall and the ceiling above it is a patch of damp. And this patch makes a shape on the wall which could be the exact shadow of the plant.

Picasso cannot forgive this habit that reality has of giving us lessons in all sorts of circumstances and in every corner. '*We don't want that interfering as well*', he says ' *or it'll be the end of everything.*'

## THAT'S WHAT OUGHT TO BE PAINTED

'*That's what ought to be painted.*' Picasso says this about thousands of sights. The street. The sea. The people. The countryside. Everything is worth painting. But two things are lacking.

'*Time*', he says, '*since you can't do everything, and you're always doing something else.*'

And then, he says, '*the means*'.

We were sitting in the open air in front of a restaurant. All through dinner, thirty feet away, a man of whom we could see nothing but the nape of his neck was talking, talking to a woman whose head rested on her hand and her elbow on the table. Picasso said:

'*And all we can do to express all that is to say: "what a lot of trouble he's taking!"* . . .'

## THE PAINTER AND HIS DATE

The conversation turned on Caravaggio.

The only thing which annoys me about him is that before we admire him we have to specify that he painted at the end of the sixteenth or the beginning of the seventeenth century. We never have to inquire into Rembrandt's birth-date. He reigns for all time without any need for historical precision.

'*But if Rembrandt were to sit down in front of you and paint your portrait*', said Picasso, '*a Rembrandt portrait exactly as he used to paint them, would you think it was good or bad?*'

Not so easy to answer. Jacqueline said:

'The only thing we could say is "Why, there's a Rembrandt we've never seen before."'

Picasso said:

'*That's right! or else "That chap really paints magnificent fake Rembrandts."* '

It was a ridiculous idea.

'*Not at all*', said Picasso. '*It also means that it's the painting that gives the date. And not at all the date that explains the painting.*'

## PERSONALITY

Picaso says:

'What I find horrible nowadays is that people are always trying to find a personality for themselves. Nobody bothers about what you might call a painter's ideal ... the kind that's always existed (I say ideal because that's what comes nearest to it). No. They couldn't care less about that.

'All they're trying to do is to make the world a present of their personality. It's horrible.

'Besides, if you're trying to find something, it means you haven't got it. And if you find it simply by looking for it, that means it's false.

'For my part, I can't do anything else but what I am doing.'

## PAINTERS AND AMBITION

We hear about certain painters of today (they've always existed, but perhaps a bit more nowadays) who use painting like a race-horse and flog it all their lives until they get to the winning-post. Then they've 'arrived' ... Or else they fall before they reach the winning-post. Picasso says:

'That's fine. Why not? The pity is that they're painters. When you're ambitious in an office, all well and good. You end up as the boss. The worst of it for painters is that they end up as ... what? ... And at the last they're not even painters any more ...'

## THE GHOST

'Here's Cézanne coming', says Picasso. 'He hasn't changed. In consequence he's still the same Cézanne. He'll do something quite different from what most people are doing. And once more nobody will notice that it's Cézanne.'

## FLAWLESS PAINTING

A long and laborious discussion on the painting of today, the strangeness of which, Picasso says, consists in the fact that it is 'flawless'.

'Take any canvas. It's good, or it's bad. It doesn't matter. But it's flawless.'

He says that for the impressionists it was quite a different matter. Because they had nevertheless a point of reference. For example Rouen cathedral. And not at any time you like; at a certain time in the afternoon. Whereas today there's nothing. No point of reference, no flaws. Very good. Even if it's very bad. Anyway you can neither correct it and so make it better, nor spoil it. It is as it is . . . And that's the flaw . . .

## THE FRENCH HOLE

A conversation of Picasso's with Pignon about the famous attacks made from all sides on French painting, or painting done in France.

They say that these attacks are inevitable from the moment

that nothing in the conception of painting prevents a painter in Tokyo, New York or Rome from doing—better or worse—the same thing as a painter in Paris. And that has been going on for years.

'*If somebody makes a hole in a canvas in America*', says Picasso, '*there's no reason for giving the prize to the French hole . . . Art is for everybody.*'

'That's what makes all the difference', says Pignon. 'Nobody could paint like Cézanne or Van Gogh. Or even Gauguin. They were the only ones.'

'*Nobody could paint like Matisse*', says Picasso. '*Nobody except Matisse could do it . . .*'

## TWELVE PICTURES IN ONE
## ONE PICTURE IN TWELVE

March 1965. Picasso was wondering what to exhibit in the Salon de Mai. He had painted an enormous number of heads of men, while at the same time continuing to paint 'The painter and his model' in a manner that had already nothing to do with the others in the series (which was six months old, and there had been vast quantities in the interval).

Picasso lined up his canvases on the ground, shoulder to shoulder. Jacqueline was constantly bringing fresh ones, and Pignon traced in the studio a maze of canvases standing up in rows. We could see them all at once. On the far wall everything was dominated by a row of heads; these ones were all painted on the same canvas. As though, sitting in the front row of the arena, they were watching our corrida of canvases.

But with the men's heads painted one by one, a canvas to each, we made some extraordinary rows of heads. '*That's how they ought to be hung*', said Picasso. Why not?

They at once began to make up a picture with quantities of

103

canvases of heads in two superimposed rows. They spent hours on it. They tried nudes and painters in the spaces between the heads, and effortlessly put themselves in too. It went on until at last they had finished their hit-or-miss jigsaw puzzle, and it seemed as though nothing more could be changed without spoiling the whole thing.

'It's a mystery', said Picasso. '*This morning not one of them even knew that the others existed.*'

The chosen ones were mounted together, and for the Salon de Mai they were given the name of 'Twelve pictures in one, one picture in twelve'.

## THE ABSTRACT HUNTER

Picasso says:

'*Imagine, for example, a hunter in the abstract. What can he do, this abstract hunter? ... In any case he won't kill anything.*'

## THE OUTSTRETCHED HAND

'*Les Horaces, by David*', says Picasso.

And his first remarks about it are enough to turn the air blue.

But it doesn't really matter. '*You can say as much as you like about it, and a bit more*', he says. '*And worse. Besides, it's easy to talk.*

'*But all the same, those outstretched hands had to be painted, and they had to be hands, and outstretched, and he had to make them exist. And after all that's what he's done.*'

104

## INNOCENCE

'What joy it must have been', says Picasso, 'to be an impressionist. They were painters in their painter's innocence.'

## THE LANDSCAPE HUNG

Picasso painted a landscape from the one he can see from his studio, a vast one, with the circle of the sea looking like a lake in the background, the towering blocks of flats, the sky. It was a rose-pink landscape. He brought it into the room he generally uses when he is not working or sleeping, and hung it on a communicating door. On its right the parrot from Gaboon. On its left the television. Under the landscape he placed, on a sloping framework, some ceramic tiles which when put together formed a man. Picasso looked kindly on this and said yes, this fellow had perhaps something in him.

What I myself liked was the rose-pink landscape with its circle of sea and its towering blocks of flats, and I said so. I said I liked that landscape.

'I don't at all', said Picasso. 'I think it's horrible. And I haven't hung it up there because I like it. On the contrary. I thought it was so bad that I brought it down as an exhibit for the prosecution. And I'm going to hang it by the neck until it's dead ...'

## THE ARISTOCRACY

'At that time,' says Picasso, 'we had no other preoccupation but what we were doing. And all the people who were doing it saw nobody but each other. Apollinaire, Max Jacob, Salmon ... Think of it, what an aristocracy!'

## THE BEACH, THE ENEMY

Time passes, people pass. There is a huge ship in the distance. Time moves slowly, as it always does on the beach. A huge ship is sailing out of the harbour. We watch until at last there is nothing left of it. The sun is setting. Everything drags and crawls in the blissful indolence of the beach, everything goes on and on and fades out and is ready to come to a halt. Picasso said in one such moment that one ought to paint a picture with time in it. But since time, in short, is simply the amount of time a painter can put into one canvas or a hundred, what one has to do is to stay in the studio and above all not to set foot on the beach.

## THE COUP DE GRACE

'Nine times out of ten, when a painter says to you: "No, that canvas isn't quite finished ... there's a little something missing ... I'll have to finish it off ..." nine times out of ten you can be sure that in order to finish it off ... well, he'll finish it off. You know, the way they finish off people executed by a firing-squad. With a revolver-shot in the head.'

106

## THE PAINTER AND THE CAMERA

You can film a man writing. The writer writes in front of the camera. He poses in front of the camera, and nobody can see what he is writing; except perhaps in close-up, a line written in his hand. For the camera. The writer and the camera are allergic one to the other. They cancel each other out. They are like reporters inventing news-stories about each other.

People believe *a priori* that a painter can be filmed with perfect truth, since what he paints can be clearly seen the moment he paints it. People think the camera can catch the painter. And really it can do nothing of the sort. But that isn't its fault.

The camera, that stabbing eye, destroys by its mere presence the indispensable element of true creation: solitude.

However, once we accept that everything hangs on the camera we can imagine a combination of painting and photography. The camera can be used for painting and painting for the cinema. That is what Picasso envisaged and Clouzot carried out in 'Le Mystère Picasso'.

'Le Mystère Picasso' was not concerned with laying bare the mystery of Picasso's painting; it was concerned with showing what Picasso could reveal in painting using the means provided by the cinema, and what the cinema could invent if it took as starting-point a man painting in front of it and for its benefit.

It would have been possible to go even further in this field. Perhaps we will one day. At any rate there were passages in this film which, though they had of necessity nothing to do with the painter at work, found their own magic compounded of painting and cinema, and then took on a dazzling beauty which came as near to creation as it possibly could . . . That was the splendid paradox of 'Le Mystère Picasso'.

We can imagine a camera hidden in the studio of a painter

who is painting. Only this, we may believe, if the painter knows nothing about it, can express the truth of the painter.

And yet it cannot, any more that anything else. All we will ever have is one single truth: that of the creative gesture, the living person, the worker in action. And even then, only provided the film as it runs is given the time it needs, which is the painter's own . . .

And yet the most wonderful moments were not those when the canvas, as if by magic, was of its own accord transformed on the screen, when the colour changed and the figures moved; and yet that was magnificent. The greatest beauty, truth, and life rested in the line that slid forward, crept and flew over the transparent paper with the sound of Picasso's pencil moving.

It was he who had thought up all the arrangements of transparent paper behind which, unseen, he drew or painted in coloured inks while the camera filmed this painting as it took shape by itself, without a painter.

It was not a painting lesson nor the revelation of a secret. When for example Clouzot filmed every five or ten minutes, or at longer or shorter intervals, the reading or sleeping woman on which Picasso was working in the meantime, the play of colours which the camera produced, changing and superimposing them one upon the other, or the movements of the coloured paper resting on or around Jacqueline, or the mysterious brushstrokes by which the red or blue was spread became, even apart from the painting, a sort of witch ballet full of a strangely moving charm. Picasso's art lay in finding what best fitted this ballet. And doing it. In front of the camera.

For those who saw this film being made, the pictures to which it gave birth will always be something apart. The dozens of mysterious, unknown canvases which had life only as long as they were being painted, and disappeared in sequence as Picasso's work went on, are for them forever locked away within the others. They do not even realize that we could say the same for nine out of ten of all the canvases in the world. But in 'Le Mystère Picasso' the camera played in relation to Picasso a part which had a diabolical fascination for him. The canvas he was painting became at once everything he was capable of doing on canvas—which means everything—and at the same time something other than painting, since he knew that the camera was recording every one of the transformations he inflicted or bestowed upon his canvas.

And these transformations came to life. They became themselves a sort of cinema-painting. The canvas was populated, and then depopulated again. Characters came in and out, stood up, lay down. The cinema acted upon painting and painting acted for the cinema. It was extraordinary.

As I recall this I am thinking especially of the canvas of La Garoupe.

La Garoupe is a resort where Picasso used to go and bathe that summer.

And all the images of a beach which he had seen there came one after another to play on the beach of his canvas in front of the camera. The figures stood up, lay down, went into the sea, sat at tables, opened beach umbrellas, practised water-skiing, swam, disappeared, flung themselves about . . . A beach with all its unbridled movement shimmered restlessly beneath the blinding light of the cameras, and we watched it from the shadowy depths of the airless claustrophobic film studio of La Victorine in August.

There was one memorable moment when in the midst of this inferno of heat, painting and cinema, we heard an aeroplane flying in the sky above. Nice. At that very second an aeroplane appeared in the sky above the beach under Picasso's brush.

He didn't want to be filmed. But he always said that marvellous things could be done with the cinema. And he did them.

That day painting acted for the screen, inventing aspects of itself exactly suited to the screen. It used time, the infinitely shifting decomposition of images, and noise.

It wasn't painting that was filmed. Painting made the film.

On the other hand—and it is a strange thing—all the canvases created in the film, for the film, by the film, because of the film, are not alive only on the screen; they never have the horrible look that marionettes have when we see them lying motionless in the intervals of puppet shows.

The canvases are alive; they really exist. They are canvases and drawings by Picasso, and the uninformed visitor could not for a second suspect that they were born in the glare of the footlights, far from the solitary places. They exist, and they hold their position.

In a word, he painted these canvases. They have not suffered from their strange birth, conditioned, closely observed and public though it was. They are simply themselves, in the face of everything.

That too is a part of the Mystère Picasso.


## PICASSO AND MATISSE

One day, on the way back from a trip into the mountains, we stopped at Vence to see Matisse's chapel.

Picasso had been there only once, while Matisse was still working on it.

He did not come to this chapel as a sightseer. He came as though to his friend's house. He was deeply moved.

At the end of a corridor an old nun was selling postcards. She answered Picasso rudely when he bought catalogues from her. But a visitor recognized him and said, wonderingly: 'What luck! I come to see Matisse and at the same time I meet Picasso!'

'Is this Picasso?' said the old nun.

She came quickly out of her hole, bent almost double, and said to Picasso:

'I didn't recognize you because I'm so old! But I'm very glad to see you because I've something to tell you. It's something Monsieur Matisse said to me when he was showing me his paintings in the chapel. He said: "I don't really know what to think about them, but at any rate there is only one person who has the right to criticise me, and that's Picasso."'

## NATURE IN TUBES

We were driving through a dazzling landscape. Sun. Meadows. Olive trees. Lakes and cypresses. Mountains.

Picasso said *'The terrible thing is that there's not one of these colours that you can buy in tubes. They'll sell you thousands of greens, Veronese green and emerald green and cadmium green and any sort of green you like; but that particular green, never.'*

## MODERN PAINTING

Picasso says: *'We must constantly realise that earlier, at the time of the impressionists or Cézanne, modern painting was something you never saw. Or else when people did open their eyes to it, it caused a scandal ... Today, provided it doesn't look like anything that could really be called painting, everything is modern, and it's staring you in the face, and as soon as it even appears it's a work of genius, and all the rest doesn't*

111

*even exist. As though people had suddenly become so percep-*
*tive that they know all about it as soon as it has even begun to*
*take shape. Whereas in reality they see precisely as they al-*
*ways did or even worse. Because now they see in exactly the*
*same way, but they imagine they've learnt to see properly.'*

## CÉZANNE AND THE STEAM ENGINE

I was talking about a lecture I heard in Paris, and about various articles I had read dealing with the great changes which
have taken place in painting in recent times. They said that
paint in pots, and brushes, were obsolete, canvases too, and all
really modern art uses objects, materials, neon etc. Painting in
oils on canvas, in an era of space-ships and sky-scraper flats, is
no longer conceivable, and so on . . .

Why not? I said. There's a whole lot of interesting things
in all this hotch-potch. But why call it painting? Let them
draw with neon and magnetic tapes and various objects—
with irons and ironing-boards too, if they like. Why not? And
others can get on with painting. It's exactly as though people
had blamed Cézanne for not painting with a steam-engine in
the glorious era of its invention.

Picasso said: 'Not at all. From the point of view of reality,
what Cézanne was doing was far more advanced than the
steam-engine.'

## JUPITER AND THETIS

Picasso was drawing on sketch-blocks placed on a chair in his
studio. He drew heads, nudes, groups, and finally some 'Jupi-

ter and Thetis' drawings inspired by the famous canvas by Ingres in the Museum at Aix-en-Provence, in which a tiny Thetis stretches out her hand to stroke the beard of an enormous and truly Olympian Jupiter.

Picasso said: '*It ought to be done life-size.*' Why not? It isn't such an enormous canvas. '*No. It's Jupiter I'd like to do life-size*', said Picasso.

## WITHOUT CANVAS OR BRUSHES

In the 1966 Salon de Mai we noticed what a great part was played by the exponents of assemblage, pop-art, op-art, and the combination of objects and materials. It was all very lively, had nothing whatever to do with painting, and was rather too reminiscent of a fairground for the more austere. The star turn was a tree, just as it was, in a pot. You saw photos of it everywhere.

We lunched in the garden and told each other all about it. Picasso and Pignon were playing with glasses, plates, cups of coffee, apples and nectarines, saying 'Here's something for the Salon de Mai.'

Finally they decided that the table, exactly as it was (and every one of the trees or the fishes in the garden), would make an entry for the Salon de Mai. No need to move anything. Nothing more to be done.

Picasso said: '*And what's more, it's so much less tiring than painting on canvas with brushes! . . .*'

## SOLITUDE

Picasso was looking at an extraordinary canvas, a 'Chateau Noir' by Cézanne, which formed part of his collection.

He said: '*And those men lived in unbelievable solitude, which was perhaps a blessing to them, even if it was their misfortune too. Is there anything more dangerous than sympathetic understanding? Especially as it doesn't exist. It's almost always wrong. You think you aren't alone. And really you're more alone than you were before.*'

## THE REAL NUDE

Picasso said to Pignon: '*You paint washers-up and more washers-up, always washers-up. But is one single one of them a real washer-up? Just as he is? No. I paint, let's say, women, or heads. Women, women, women. And yet can you say that it's Woman, just as she is? No. What I should like to do is to paint Woman as she is, or your head as it is . . . And that's what I've got to do . . .*'

## SOMETHING THEY'VE NEVER SEEN

*Nowadays people talk about painting in the same way as they do about mini-skirts. Next season it'll be longer, or it'll have a fringe on . . . We want something they've never seen. Something that'll really puzzle them. But when you look for that something, everybody's already seen it, everywhere, with a crease in its trousers.*

114

ONLY ONCE

*You can try anything in painting. You even have a right to.
Provided you never do it again.*

TRUTH

*If there were only one truth, you couldn't paint a hundred
canvases on the same theme.*

# Postface

## SUCCESS AND GLORY

The world has never known a painter so laden with glory. He has the glory of his painting and that of his personality. The glory of art galleries and the glory of nations. His face is as well-known as his name. In the streets of Cannes or Paris he is more of a star than any star of the screen. When he walks in the streets of Marseilles, too, it is a popular event. The glory of the 'Demoiselles d'Avignon' and the widespread fame of the 'Dove', Cubism and 'Guernica', the nudes and the wars, the bulls and the heroes . . . all this added to a life that has become a legend, an appearance exceptionally photogenic, a hundred thousand stories and anecdotes in which true and false are inextricably mixed, a hundred thousand pictures, tapestries, scarves, stained glass, engravings on cement, iron statues, carpets, published collections of ceramics, etc . . . etc . . . taken from the originals; thousands of articles, studies, books, all existing on the fringes of an immense output of canvases, drawings, etchings, lithographs, linocuts, ceramics, sculptures in stone, bronze or iron, etc . . . etc . . .

In short, glory.

Painters have been fêted in Florence, in Rome, and in all the courts of the Renaissance, but never to this extent. There have been painters showered with wealth, whose signature was worth their weight in gold. But never as much as this. Picasso's hand, which once grasped the dry crusts of his Montmartre days, now transforms into riches everything that it signs.

His name has passed into popular speech. Everything that hasn't a nose and mouth like you and me, everything brightly

coloured, or incomprehensible, or caricatural, in fact anything not photographic in painting, is 'Picasso'. Film studios
have quantities of Picasso reproductions for hanging on the
walls of rooms on the screen. The heroes of thrillers talk about
him and he is discussed by the kids in strip cartoons. All over
the world people talk about possessing Picassos, painting like
Picasso or not like Picasso, being or not being Picasso. In 1965
Picasso had an operation; and had to resort to the most devious
tactics in order to conceal this event successfully. You can
imagine what would otherwise have happened.

A star, then—though without worldliness—the subject of
everyone's curiosity, the centre of all sorts of financial
interests, fair game for photographers and film-makers and
newshounds, the dream of every art gallery curator, the cher-
ished jewel of every collector, this man who, moreover, has
always shared in the life of his times and taken sides on all
occasions—with the risk of attack from every quarter—knows
a glory more exalted, more immense, more universal, more
general, more immoderate, than any other painter in the
world has ever known.

This is what we must first determine if we want to give an
idea of the climate in which Picasso lives today.

First of all—glory.

All this leads us to believe that in spite of everything the
situation of painters has changed; that the world has now more
insight and no longer suffers from the blind spots which made
it ignore Van Gogh and spit on Manet.

And yet if we look at things more closely, we perceive that
nothing has changed. It's always exactly the same painter.
And exactly the same crowd. It is simply that things strike us
differently.

First of all, people don't like glory, and never have. What
we call the public—that strange mixture made up of the
accumulated readers of every newspaper for every different
social class; cultured or uncultured; conditioned for the benefit

of people who turn out newspapers with or without reserve, but generally without; product of all the modern techniques of information, deformation and the simultaneous mass-production of truth and lies; this blend of ingenuousness which will swallow anything, and intellectual snobbery which takes up whatever modern idea is in fashion—what we call 'the public' views glory with curiosity but not with respect. On the contrary. Nothing pleases it more than to witness attacks on a glittering name; it is the only characteristic to show that a little of the Greek remains in us.

Generalities apart, this public has an old score to settle with Picasso. Whatever we may say, write or do, this public is still the one for whom Picasso is a man who set out to 'make fools of everyone' by his painting. For years and years—and still today in many cases—the burning question, asked in the most unexpected quarters—I mean where it seemed most inexplicable—was 'Is he, or isn't he, a humbug?' I challenge absolutely anybody to say he hasn't heard that question a thousand times in his life. (And he's lucky if it has remained a question). Obviously one could always fall back on the 'Dove' (and even there he hasn't entirely escaped unpleasantness). And the 'Dove', in all his immense output of painting, was no more than one or two very small birds . . .

Even so, if he had always stayed the same, people would have got used to it. If he had remained a cubist or a derivative painter, they could have ended by liking him quite safely. If all his life he had painted full-face portraits with the nose in profile and one eye vertical, it would finally—with rather more difficulty—have been accepted. But he is always changing. When another 'Guernica' was expected, he painted 'War and Peace'. And when people fell in love with 'War and Peace', he did a painting for UNESCO which aroused the public's anger yet again. Until it calmed down. And so on. As soon as he has finished something he looks for something different. His glory comes, too, from that constant renewal which has always set him in the forefront of his time. But that same renewal has made him eternally alone. We must

118

always get to know him. And so always get to know him afresh.

It is hard to be lonely, as Van Gogh knew—even to death. But it is no easier to be a daily target. And not one of the compensations that glory brings can cure the wounds inflicted in our own time.

The best-known example, and unfortunately one of the most recent—since a new wave of Papini-disease has broken out very recently—is that of the Picasso of Papini, an Italian writer who amused himself by inventing imaginary interviews with Hitler or Molotov and imaginary revelations on Goethe or Kafka, Cervantes or Walt Whitman. In his book entitled *Il Libro Nero*, Giovanni Papini published among others an article called : 'Visit to Picasso (or the End of Art)'.

According to this article he went to Antibes to see Picasso, who made him a complete confession in the following vein: nobody was interested in art any more, young people liked nothing but machines and sport, etc . . . etc . . . It would be too hard and too 'dangerous from the subsistence point of view' (sic) to change his profession. Fortunately there were still 'people of refinement, the idle rich, and those who wish to extract every drop of experience from life' who were after anything 'new, strange, original, extravagant or scandalous' . . .

'As far as I'm concerned', says Papini's Picasso, 'from the very beginning I've satisfied these gentlemen and the critics with all the oddities I could think of; the less they understand, the more they admire. By dint of indulging in these little games—all these circus tricks, puzzles, brain-twisters and acrobatics—I became famous quite rapidly. Fame for a painter means sales, profits, fortune, wealth . . . I'm only a public entertainer who has understood the age he lives in and exploited as best he could the stupidity, vanity and greed of his contemporaries.' Etc . . . Etc.

You may wonder why I attach such importance to so trivial

a theme. But nevertheless I must emphasise the fact that this text was published in a book which purported to give in its preface the key to these pathetic imaginary visits.

No sooner was the book published than the whole world was reproducing the interview of Picasso by Papini with indignation and derision. But this time the interview was no longer imaginary; it was presented as a real interview.

An Italian journalist, Leonardo Borgese, wrote to Papini in 1952 to ask for an exact reply to all the questions which occurred to him. This is the letter (hitherto unpublished) in which Papini replied (1):

'The visit to Picasso—like all the rest of the book—is invented and imaginary. But this chapter was translated into French and published as an interview in a newspaper, appearing shortly after, in every country of Europe and America, arousing considerable approbation, doubts, incredulity and controversy. And there are many people who believe that this conversation with Picasso is authentic' . . .

But what matters is the effect produced by 'Picasso's confession to Papini'. The story broke for the first time in 1952 and 1953, when the 'Libro Nero' came out. A whole section of the press and public was exultant; Picasso had confessed, and proved them right; that was just what they'd always said. They congratulated themselves, gloating. The text was published, among others, by serious art periodicals. People of high intellectual ability took notice of it.

The second phase of the disease, only two years ago, was much more serious. Suddenly 'Picasso's confession' broke once more into print, in magazines and newspapers all over the world. It was held up as a triumph, and thrown in the face of Picasso's admirers. 'You've been had', they said. 'This proves it! He's confessed!'

Polish, Hungarian and Yugoslavian newspapers took it up in turn. The 'confession' was even stopped at the moment

---

1 Leonardo Borgese himself communicated this document to me.

when it was about to appear officially in the Soviet Union, where it would certainly have greatly delighted many people.

'Picasso admits: "I am only a public entertainer"' was the usual headline.

We can well imagine the bitterness with which Picasso saw his false confession circling the world like wildfire.

It is a strange thing that of all Papini's imaginary texts, this was the only one that was ever taken as authentic. There were no others.

This outrageous story is one of the most characteristic of these last few years. It means that Picasso, whatever his glory, continued to be branded and misunderstood, as the symbol not only of everything glorious, but above all of everything modern. This was the old eternal hate of all that is new or *avant-garde*, all that turns accepted notions upside down in the search for unknown truths.

Another characteristic example of Picasso's present position in the world is that of the book which a woman who had lived with him for ten years published first in America, then in France and elsewhere.

For the first time in his life, Picasso set his face against a text which concerned him, and took legal action against it, so that his position on the subject might be clarified for the present and the future. In the age of Picasso, Picasso in person discredited a book which concerned him.

On two occasions the law upheld the book against Picasso. And with it the greater part of the press, in opposition to the painters, writers, men of the theatre and persons of culture who took up arms for Picasso.

No, nothing has changed.

Picasso too says so when he looks back on his strange and difficult life. It is a life made up of great contrasts. He is flattered and congratulated to his face and immediately stabbed in the back. He is admired. And he is betrayed. People flock to his exhibitions and make a fuss of him. And at the same time a thousand '*sufferings from spite*' (the phrase is his own) are heaped one upon the other. Nothing is given to him freely, he gains nothing, obtains nothing, without a struggle. He has to begin again and again. As in painting.

Perhaps this reverse side of glory is a good thing. Perhaps in the long run Picasso is himself only in this war he must wage perpetually, bearing at the same time the further suffering born of his own glory.

It is no unjustified glory like that of certain painters who are fashionable for a time, or pseudo-modern, or who adapt themselves to artistic trends instead of setting them. Picasso's glory cannot fade. For it rests upon an immense body of work. He pays for it dearly. But it is there.

This man, whose tempestuous life has been tossed by every whirlwind, tortured by a thousand problems concerned or not concerned with painting, filled with brief hours snatched from painting, has set and still sets the example of strict uninterrupted work. For long periods he is utterly lost in thought. He lives by his passions in the direct line of his brother painters. Like them he knows the joy of creating truth, and their crucifixions are his also. Even if they seem very different, they are the same.

I've seen Picasso in the lovely town of Arles, storming through hotel corridors full of reproductions of Van Gogh. Postcards of Van Gogh's little room were pinned up in the bedrooms. '*That makes it all so much more cruel*', said Picasso.

He cherishes a photo-copy he had made of four short lines in a contemporary newspaper, reporting, between the theft of a basket of fish and some dog run over in Arles, that a man by the name of Van Gogh was admitted to hospital because he had cut off his ear.

All this simply means that in this vast Picasso-world, in the chaos of all that is said and written on the subject, in this glory which is never success, in this medley of ideas, truths and

counter-truths, woven around works which have revolution-
ized painting since this century began, and around a man
whose slightest movement calls up a thousand commentaries,
true, false or ecstatic, there is, above and before everything
else, alone, bound up with the world yet utterly dedicated to
his creative function, a painter. A man of painting. Given over
to painting, body and soul. A painter among painters, whose
natural and indispensable element is painting. For him it is
religion. Necessity. Greatness. Conquest. And punishment.

This is the painter of whom I have tried to evoke a direct
image. In any case, a true one.

## GEORGE ALLEN & UNWIN LTD
London: 40 Museum Street, W.C.1

Auckland: P.O. Box 36013, Northcote Central, N.4
Barbados: P.O. Box 222, Bridgetown
Beirut: Deeb Building, Jeanne d'Arc Street
Bombay: 15 Graham Road, Ballard Estate, Bombay 1
Buenos Aires: Escritorio 454–459, Florida 165
Calcutta: 17 Chittaranjan Avenue, Calcutta 13
Cape Town: 68 Shortmarket Street
Hong Kong: 105 Wing On Mansion, 26 Hancow Road, Kowloon
Ibadan: P.O. Box 62
Karachi: Karachi Chambers, McLeod Road
Madras: Mohan Mansions, 38c Mount Road, Madras 6
Mexico: Villalongin 32, Mexico 5, D.F.
Nairobi: P.O. Box 30583
New Delhi: 13–14 Asaf Ali Road, New Delhi 1
Ontario: 81 Curlew Drive, Don Mills
Philippines: P.O. Box 4322, Manilla
Rio de Janeiro: Caixa Postal 2537–Zc–00
Singapore: 36c Prinsep Street, Singapore 7
Sydney, N.S.W.: Bradbury House, 55 York Street
Tokyo: P.O. Box 26, Kamata

*Rubens and his Times*
ROGER AVERMAETE

TRANSLATED BY CHRISTINE TROLLOPE

After eight years in foreign parts, a painter came back to settle in a country ravaged by years of war. He had left at the very beginning of his career, and when he returned he was thirty-three years old. Immediately he took his place as a leader, easily outshining all the other painters, numerous as they were, who worked in the town in which he had come to live. Commissions flowed in, and pupils too. The cleverest craftsmen used their special skills to collaborate with him, and in accepting their assistance he changed their whole conception of their art and drew them effortlessly into his own Dionysian world. Once he had decided to take an active part in politics, he became a diplomat despite the opposition of those who ended by employing him. He became rich and respected; honours were conferred upon him, kings, princes, ministers were his friends. For some thirty years a strict self-imposed discipline kept at bay the lust for power he felt within himself. And although he spent his last years in the peace of the countryside like any great lord to whom the years have brought some measure of disillusionment, it can only have been because he coveted the supreme delight of savouring and rejecting all the vanity of worldly pomp.

Such a man was Rubens. He strove after success, and his career is one of the most amazingly successful ever known. Much has been written about him; his work has been studied with fervour, clarity and enthusiasm. His biographers have been legion, but Rubens' work has always befogged them so that they show an irritating tendency towards exaggeration, and legend has taken precedence over history. Roger Avermaete, a Fleming himself, has written this new biography in the modern and more balanced style: factually informative and intensely readable, it creates, in addition, an unforgettable portrait of a man whose radiance made the colourless reign of the Archduke Albert pass for a golden age, and whose vitality and versatility make even his many brilliant contemporaries seem by comparison to be of small stature.

## The Essential Vasari

Abridged and edited by BETTY BURROUGHS

Giorgio Vasari, the devoted friend of Michelangelo and himself an artist, lived in the thick of the Italian Renaissance. His book, *Lives of the Most Eminent Architects, Painters and Sculptors of Italy*, is one of those inexhaustible and irreplaceable treasure-chests, originally in five volumes, packed with detailed information, criticism, and anecdotes, dramatic and amusing, of popes, princes, merchants, and craftsmen of every kind. To read him is to experience the Renaissance and share in its quarrels and generosities, its magnificence and intrigue, its ferment and glory. For this edition twenty-five of the best-known Lives have been selected, including those of Giotto, Botticelli, Leonardo da Vinci, Raphael, Titian, and, of course, Michelangelo.

## History of Mankind Vol VI

WARE, PANNIKAR and ROMEIN

The first half of the twentieth century has witnessed spectacular developments in the history of mankind. This volume describes the transformation wrought by the revolutionary political and social changes of this period, and by the impact of scientific knowledge on industry, communications, transport, food, health, human behaviour and on warfare. The half-century has also witnessed a gradual shift in the centre of world power from nineteenth-century Europe to the United States and the Soviet Union; it has seen the emergence of new nations in Asia and Africa from colonial or semi-colonial status; the crystallization of nationalism and the beginnings of international co-operation; the increasing power of the state and rival forms of organization; fundamental changes in attitude towards labour relations, the status of women, racial minorities, and other class and caste groups.

Significant too have been developments in the scientific field, which by mid-century have brought a further scientific revolution; changes in social institutions, the role of religion, education, and the cultural implications of the enormously increasing opportunities for leisure. This volume also throws light on the national aspirations which have provided the motive power for peoples in many parts of the world, and on the interacting influence of art and literature and the exchange of ideas during a period which has seen the opening up of hitherto undreamed of potentialities for the well-being and also the destruction of mankind.

LONDON: GEORGE ALLEN AND UNWIN

## The Autobiography of Bertrand Russell

The publication of the first part of Bertrand Russell's autobiography was a literary event of the greatest importance, and the praise it received was universal. *Sir Denis Brogan* in *The Glasgow Herald* described it as 'One of the most astonishing and almost totally gratifying performances I at any rate have read for a good many years'. *Michael Foot* (in *The Evening Standard*) said that it was 'Hilarious and deeply moving, sharp and beautiful . . . something better than a book in a million. The Hero is unique.' 'Splendid', 'riveting', 'fascinating', 'astonishing', 'remarkable', are typical of the terms used in the hundreds of full-length reviews that quickly accumulated. Before publication the publishers themselves ventured the view that this autobiography would prove comparable in significance with that of Rousseau, and this opinion seems to have been supported widely.

The second part carries the reader from the outbreak of the First World War till almost the end of the Second. It is a period of the greatest significance in the author's life and also in world history. As he says himself: 'My life before 1910 and my life after 1914 were as sharply separated as Faust's life before and after he met Mephistopheles.' In this book we read how the War shook Russell out of his prejudices and made him think afresh on fundamental questions. We see the effect of this fresh thinking on his public actions and his personal relations. He lost old friends and made new ones; he moved in new directions; he began to write a new kind of book; his whole conception of human nature changed. He joined energetically in the campaign for peace, which culminated in his imprisonment in 1918. After the war he journeyed through post-revolutionary Russia, and he travelled through China and took up teaching there. He married a second and a third time. He wrote a whole series of famous books which began with *The Principals of Social Reconstruction* and ended with *The History of Western Philosophy*, with works like *Marriage and Morals* in between. He founded a school. He established a family. He taught in America and was the victim of a typical witch-hunt. And through the pages move many new characters, like Lytton Strachey, D. H. Lawrence, Gilbert Murray, T. S. Eliot, J. M. Keynes, Katherine Mansfield, Constance Malleson, besides some who appeared in the first volume.

LONDON: GEORGE ALLEN AND UNWIN